W9-AEY-073

ETHNOGRAPHIC SURVEY OF AFRICA

EDITED BY DARYLL FORDE

EAST CENTRAL AFRICA

PART V

THE KIKUYU AND KAMBA OF KENYA

BY

JOHN MIDDLETON
and
GREET KERSHAW

LONDON

INTERNATIONAL AFRICAN INSTITUTE

1965

Price 20s. net

ETHNOGRAPHIC SURVEY OF AFRICA

EDITED BY DARYLL FORDE

EAST CENTRAL AFRICA

PART V

THE CENTRAL TRIBES OF THE NORTH-EASTERN BANTU

ETHNOGRAPHIC SURVEY OF AFRICA

EDITED BY DARYLL FORDE

EAST CENTRAL AFRICA

PART V

THE CENTRAL TRIBES OF THE NORTH-EASTERN BANTU

(The Kikuyu, including Embu, Meru, Mbere, Chuka, Mwimbi, Tharaka, and the Kamba of Kenya)

BY

JOHN MIDDLETON
and
GREET KERSHAW

LONDON

INTERNATIONAL AFRICAN INSTITUTE

1965

This section of the Ethnographic Survey of Africa was first published in 1953 with the aid of a grant made by the Secretary of State, under the Colonial Development and Welfare Acts, on the recommendation of the Colonial Social Science Research Council.

Revised Edition 1965

Printed in Great Britain by The Sidney Press Ltd, Bedford

FOREWORD

THE International African Institute has, since 1945, been engaged on the preparation and publication of an Ethnographic Survey of Africa, the purpose of which is to present in a brief and readily comprehensible form a summary of available information concerning the different peoples of Africa with respect to location, natural environment, economy and crafts, social structure, political organization, religious beliefs and cults. While available published material has provided the basis for the Survey, a mass of unpublished documents, reports and records in government files and in the archives of missionary societies, as well as field notes and special communications by anthropologists and others, have been generously made available and these have been supplemented by personal correspondence and consultation. The Survey is being published in a number of separate volumes, each of which is concerned with one people or a group of related peoples, and contains a comprehensive bibliography and specially drawn map.

A committee of the Institute was set up under the Chairmanship of the late Professor Radcliffe-Brown, and the Director of the Institute undertook the organization and editing of the Survey. The generous collaboration of a number of research institutions and administrative officers in Europe and the African territories was secured, as well as the services of senior anthropologists who have been good enough to supervise and amplify the drafts.

The work of the Survey was initiated with the aid of a grant from the British Colonial Development and Welfare Fund, on the recommendation of the Social Science Research Council, to be applied mainly, though not exclusively, to work relating to British territories. A further grant from the Sudan Government has assisted in the preparation and publication of sections dealing with that territory.

The Ministère de la France d'Outre-Mer and the Institute Français d'Afrique Noire were good enough to express their interest in the project, and through their good offices grants have been received from the Governments of French West Africa, the French Cameroons and French Equatorial Africa for the preparation and publication of sections relating to those areas. These sections have been prepared by French ethnologists with the support and advice of the late Professor M. Griaule of the Sorbonne, Mme. Calame-Griaule and Professor Th. Monod, Director of I.F.A.N.

The collaboration of the Belgian authorities in this project was first secured by the good offices of the late Professor de Jonghe, who enlisted the interest of the Commission d'Ethnologie of the Institut Royal Colonial Belge. The collaboration of the Institut pour la Recherche Scientifique en Afrique Centrale has also been readily accorded. Work relating to former Belgian territories is being carried out at the Centre de Documentation of the Musée de l'Afrique Centrale, Tervuren, where Mlle. Boone and members of her staff are engaged on the assembly and classification of the vast mass of material relating to African peoples in the Congo and Ruanda-Urundi. They work in close collaboration with ethnologists in the field, to whom draft manuscripts are submitted for checking.

The International African Institute desires to express its grateful thanks to those official bodies whose generous financial assistance has made the carrying out of this project possible and to the many scholars, directors of research organizations, administrative officers, missionaries, and others who have collaborated in the work and, by granting facilities to our research workers and by correcting and supervising their manuscripts, have contributed so largely to whatever merit the various sections may possess.

Since the unequal value and unsystematic nature of existing material was one of the reasons for undertaking the Survey, it is obvious that these studies cannot claim to be complete or definitive; it is hoped, however, that they will present a clear account of our existing knowledge and indicate where information is lacking and further research is needed. A list of sections already published will be found on pp. 101–3.

This part is a revised version of that published in 1953. Most of the new material in the section on the social organization and the political system has been written by Mrs. Greet Kershaw, who worked among the Kikuyu in 1955–56. We are grateful to Mr. T. G. Benson for his assistance in checking the orthography of this revised version.

DARYLL FORDE,
Director,
International African Institute.

June 1964.

CONTENTS

CONTENTS—*continued*

INTRODUCTION

The Kikuyu and Kamba are the largest of the North-east Bantu-speaking peoples, the former being the largest in East Africa. Linguistically they are closely related one to the other and to the Coastal Bantu.[1]

There is probably more literature on these peoples than on any other groups in East Africa. Little of it is the work of modern social anthropologists, although both tribes were early studied by trained ethnographers: Routledge went to Kikuyu in 1902 and Lindblom to Kamba in 1910–12. Both have at times been administered by officers who have written on them—Dundas, Hobley, Lambert, and Penwill—all of whose accounts are reliable and profuse. There are two other full-length books on the Kikuyu, one by the present Prime Minister of Kenya, Mr. Kenyatta, the other by Father Cagnolo, a Catholic missionary. The result of this mass of material is that many aspects of the cultures of these peoples have been described at great length and in considerable detail, but information as to some of the aspects of social organization which today are regarded as important, such as the territorial, clan, age-set and age-grade systems, is seriously deficient. Information as to land tenure, law, and main cultural details, however, is fairly good.

Extensive work was undertaken on some aspects of Kikuyu social organization by Mrs. Greet Kershaw during the years 1955 to 1956; this will be published in due course. The data collected by Dr. J. Fisher in 1950 were not available at the time of writing, nor is the full-length work on the Kikuyu by Dr. L. S. B. Leakey. The Northern Kikuyu tribes, living to the east and south-east of Mount Kenya, have hardly been studied: there are accounts by two administrators, Orde-Browne and Lambert, and by a missionary, Father Bernardi, and little more.

It is clear that traditional Kikuyu society was marked by extreme variation, and that much distortion has been caused in the published accounts by generalization made from small-scale studies in particular areas. In this volume the authors have therefore tried where possible not to generalize from what at first may seem inconsistent accounts. It should be mentioned that most of the published material is on the Southern Kikuyu, there being comparatively little data on the Central and Northern Kikuyu groups.

It should also be stressed that extensive changes have taken place among the Kikuyu and Kamba during this century. They have been in close contact with Europeans since the beginning of the century, and the Kikuyu especially have featured in the modern political movements in Kenya. Modern events are not dealt with in any detail in this survey of the literature. The volumes of the Ethnographic Survey deal mainly with traditional forms of culture, and in this volume emphasis is therefore placed upon the pre-colonial cultures of these peoples, in so far as it can be reconstructed. The accounts of the Kikuyu and Kamba have been written at various times since the beginning of the century. Generally the date of an account has not been taken into consideration, and the societies have been described as they seem to have been traditionally.

In recent years there has been a spate of material published on the Mau Mau movement (see the Bibliography at the end of this volume). However, there is as yet no satisfactory account of Mau Mau available, and we do not, therefore, discuss it.

[1] See Prins, 1952.

I. THE KIKUYU

TRIBAL AND SUB-TRIBAL GROUPINGS AND DEMOGRAPHY

Nomenclature and Location

The present-day Central Province of Kenya includes two Bantu-speaking groups, the Kikuyu and the Kamba. The Kikuyu[2] tribes consist of the Kikuyu proper and a cluster of smaller groups living on the eastern and southern slopes of Mount Kenya, to the north of the Kikuyu proper. They are apparently all related in physical character, culture and language.

The Kamba are dealt with separately in Section II of this volume (pp. 67–87).

The Kikuyu tribes inhabit five administrative Districts which were created by the British Government during the first quarter of this century: Kiambu, Fort Hall, Nyeri, Embu, and Meru, which stretch in a belt from south to north. Kiambu in the south is within a few miles of Nairobi, the capital of Kenya, and has been broken up into several small sections separated by the blocks of European farms on land beside the railway.[3]

Embu District is occupied by the Embu, the Mbere, the Ndia and the Kichugu, the two latter usually being referred to as the Ndia Kikuyu and Kichugu Kikuyu, who are best regarded as Kikuyu although there are slight cultural differences.

Meru District is occupied by several tribal groups: Tigania, Igembe, Imenti, Miutini, Igoji, Mwimbi, Muthambi, Tharaka and Chuka, all of which, with the exception of Tharaka and Chuka, are traditionally part of the so-called "Meru", perhaps a territorial rather than a tribal name. Igoji is closely related to Mwimbi and Muthambi, and these three as a group are regarded as being a sub-division of Imenti but territorially separated from it by the Miutini, relations of the Chuka. The Chuka are very distinct, physically and culturally, from these other groups. The Tharaka seem to have affinities with both Meru and Kamba, and Lambert suggests that they are in fact "an aggregation of offshoots . . . from various tribes, including Meru, Chuka, Mbere and Kamba".[4] Today Meru District contains five Divisions, those of Igembe, Tigania, Imenti, Tharaka and Chuka, the last containing the sections of Chuka, Miutini, Igoji, Mwimbi and Muthambi.

The southern boundary of Kikuyu is about 6,000 feet above sea level and follows the edge of the Masai plains where they give way to the wooded and well-watered hills of Kiambu. In the east Kikuyu is bounded by the Athi plains, occupied by Masai, the Ulu Hills, occupied by Kamba, and the Tana River, the boundary between Tharaka and Kamba. In the west Kikuyu stretches to the peaks of the Aberdare Range, Kinangop and Settima, which boundary between the Kikuyu and Masai has marked the administrative "reserves" of the colonial period. Only to the north-east do the wooded Kikuyu highlands continue north-wards to the Nyombeni Range, and in this north-eastern extension live the Embu and Meru. The slopes of Mount Kenya are occupied up to about 7,000 feet. North of Mount Kenya and the Nyombeni Range are the arid deserts of the Northern Frontier Province, occupied by Samburu, Boran, Somali and other Hamitic-speaking peoples.

[2] The correct designations are Mugikuyu (pl. Agikuyu) for the people, Ugikuyu for the country, and Gigikuyu for the language, but it is more convenient to use the customary spelling Kikuyu, which will refer to the Kikuyu proper only (Central and South Kikuyu: see below).

The word Kikuyu may be derived from *mukuyu* (fig-tree); (see Routledge, 1910, p. 1; Kenyatta, 1938, p. 257).

[3] The terminology is confusing, since "Kikuyu" is generally used to refer only to the inhabitants of Kiambu, Fort Hall, and Nyeri Districts. When we speak of the "Kikuyu tribes" we refer to the entire group; when we speak of "Kikuyu", we refer to the Kikuyu "proper", those of these three Districts only.

[4] Lambert, 1950, pp. 1–3; Bernardi, 1959, p. 3 ff.

The land occupied by the Kikuyu tribes is thus a geographically distinct region, consisting of the high plateau, dominated by the massifs of Mount Kenya and the Aberdares, which forms that part of the Kenya Highlands to the east of the Rift and the highlands. The plains to the north consist of lavas unsuited for agriculture; east, north-west and south the plains are suitable only for cattle-keeping, and over 7,000 feet the slopes of Mount Kenya and the Aberdares are too high to support crops.[5]

Demographic Data

The population of the Kikuyu tribes at the latest census, that taken in 1948, was as follows:[6]

District	*Tribe*	*Population*	*Area in sq. miles*[7]	*Average density per sq. mile*
Kiambu	Kikuyu	251,884	324	777
Fort Hall	,,	300,355	583	515
Nyeri	,,	179,956	336	536
Embu	Embu	61,747	1,234	163
	Mbere	29,778		
	Ndia	66,680		
	Kichugu	42,727		
Meru	Meru	198,789	1,371	188
	Mwimbi	19,020		
	Muthambi	5,491		
	Chuka	18,480		
	Tharaka	16,505		

There were also many Kikuyu dispersed in other Districts:

District	*Tribe*	*Population*
Nairobi	Kikuyu	51,475
	Embu	4,238
Thika	Kikuyu	21,439
Kitui	Meru	5,101
Nanyuki	Kikuyu	23,287
	Meru	2,921
Trans-Nzoia	Kikuyu	2,219
Uasin Gishu	Kikuyu	12,907
Nakuru	Kikuyu	130,303
Laikipia	Kikuyu	28,068
Mombasa	Kikuyu	3,304

Total Kikuyu population for Kenya in 1948 was:

Kiambu Kikuyu	388,162
Fort Hall Kikuyu	384,851
Nyeri Kikuyu	253,328
	1,026,341

[5] See Fitzgerald, 1948, p. 253; Hobley, 1938, p. 319.

[6] From published figures of the East African Census, 1948, except for figures for Meru which are from Lambert, 1950, p. 154: the Census figures are given for Locations in Meru, which do not show tribal composition. These figures show only Kikuyu living in these Districts (i.e., they exclude a small minority of immigrants and settlers of different tribal origin who live in the Districts).

[7] These figures exclude public grazing areas and forest reserves, which together come to 2,268 square miles.

It is important to note that there has been a high degree of movement of Kikuyu, both between Kikuyu districts, and between the previous Kikuyu "reserves" and Nairobi and other districts (in particular the Rift Valley areas).[8]

Figures showing the rate of increase of population in Kikuyu are not satisfactory. They are available for South Nyeri over the period 1936–1944, and show an increase from approximately 142,000 to 166,000; during this period the average annual increase of males was 2·56%. The total increase rate for the Kikuyu Districts (Kiambu, Fort Hall and Nyeri) was 1·84% per annum.[9] Figures given in the Kenya Land Commission Evidence covering the period 1921–1931 show an average annual increase of 1·5%.[10] The K.L.C. Report stated that it was estimated that at the time when the Limuru farms were alienated the average Kikuyu woman had about one acre under cultivation. This would mean that in the Kikuyu country as a whole only one acre in eight was cultivated.[11] The annual rate of increase for Embu since 1927 has been 0·6%.[12]

Neighbouring Peoples

Save in the north-east, where the Kikuyu highlands join Embu and Meru, the Kikuyu and their northern neighbours were separated by a belt of no-man's-land, only a few miles in width in Kiambu, probably wider elsewhere. This belt consisted partly of unwatered and unattractive plains and partly of thick forest, which was never cut down by the Kikuyu and was filled by them with war-pits. Von Höhnel, one of the first Europeans to traverse Kikuyu country, describes this peripheral forest belt as being one or two hours' march in depth and as extending all round Kikuyu.[13]

The Kikuyu and Masai were closely linked by both trade and cattle raiding. The Masai were invincible on their own terrain, the plains, but were easy victims for the Kikuyu if they ventured into the forests, where they were killed by the arrows and staked war-pits which awaited them. Usually, however, there were peaceful relations, and there was always much intermarriage.[14] There was also a great deal of ceremonial and ritual interdependence between these groups. There was always trade, women being able to pass freely from one to the other.[15] Stigand states that Kikuyu often "lent" their cattle to be tended by the Masai,[16] and Eliot writes that in the great famine of 1882 Masai settled in Kikuyu and took Kikuyu wives, sometimes entering the service of Kikuyu as "a sort of mercenaries".[17] It is said that alliances were made in the past between sections of the Kikuyu and neighbouring tribes; these allies included Masai groups.[18]

Traditions of Origin and History

It is generally held that there were five autochthonous peoples who occupied various parts of Kikuyu before the present inhabitants. They fall into two groups:

[8] Southall 1961, p. 168 ff.

[9] Humphrey, 1945, p. 3.

[10] K.L.C. Evidence, 1932, I, p. 976. This figure is suspect, since the figures on which it is based were taken from tax registers, not from birth registers (which did not exist), and so an allowance must be made for population movements from the north to the more wealthy south, and for improvements in registration methods. See also J. E. Goldthorpe, Appendix VII in Great Britain, *Report of the East African Royal Commission*, 1955: 462–467.

[11] K.L.C. Report, 1932, para. 68. See also para. 72.

[12] K.L.C. Evidence I, p. 538.

[13] Von Höhnel, 1894, I, pp. 302, 352.

[14] Routledge, 1910, pp. 13–14; Hobley, 1938, pp. 244–7; Thomson, 1885, p. 177; Boyes, 1911, p. 110; Kenyatta, 1938, pp. 208–11; C. Dundas, 1915, p. 236; Bugeau, 1943, p. 185.

[15] See below, p. 19; also Wakefield, 1870, p. 318.

[16] Stigand, 1913, p. 241.

[17] Eliot, 1905, p. 127.

[18] Kenyatta, 1938, p. 110 Boyes, 1911, p. 110; Hobley, 1938, p. 93; Cagnolo, 1933, pp. 101–2.

the cattle-keeping Mwoko and Njuwe, and the hunting and gathering Gumba, Aathi and Dorobo.

The Mwoko lived in the plains in Meru and the Njuwe in Tharaka; they were driven out or absorbed by the later peoples when they moved into the country from the east.[19]

The Gumba, who no longer exist, are remembered in the traditions of the Chuka, Mwimbi, Tharaka and some of the Kikuyu sections. They are said to have lived in underground pits or tunnels, the supposed remains of which have been found in almost all parts of the area. Routledge excavated several of the saucer-shaped depressions on the slopes of Mount Kenya, which are said to have been their dwellings, and found potsherds and artifacts of obsidian; Leakey has made similar excavations. The Dorobo, like the Kikuyu, use iron and have always done so as far as their traditions tell. The Kikuyu refer to them as *maitho ma ciana*, which is variously translated as "the eyes of the children" (from their shy manner), "the fierce little people" or "the enemies of the children".[20]

It is not certain that the Aathi were a separate people, and there is considerable evidence that they were Dorobo; the name *Aathi* means "hunters", so that it is possible that the name refers in general to previous hunting peoples rather than to one particular tribe.[21] Some Southern Kikuyu also state that *Aathi* means the sellers (*mwathi*, pl. *aathi*) of the land, and so refers in general to the previous inhabitants.

A considerable amount is known about the Dorobo or Okiek, who still exist in several parts of Kenya and adjacent territories, and who were being displaced by the Kikuyu within living memory. They were, and are, hunting and gathering people, without livestock. They exchanged rights over land for livestock with the Kikuyu. Intermarriage occurred, although, with the clearing of the forests by the Kikuyu and subsequent migration of game into the Mount Kenya and Aberdare massifs, most of the Dorobo either died out or moved after the game; they now live a precarious existence on the fringes of larger tribes such as Nandi, whose language most of them in Kenya have borrowed.[22]

Today the problem of the identity and history of these peoples, especially the Dorobo, has become one of great local importance, owing to the light they throw on Kikuyu land-rights.[23]

A reconstructed history of the Kikuyu has been given by Lambert. Omitting consideration of some of the smaller northern groups (especially the Chuka), he states that it may be assumed that the Mbere, Embu, Kichugu, Ndia and Kikuyu represent successive stages of settlement during a general migration from the east. He discusses tribal traditions, and attempts to date the migrations. The general direction of movement in the present area was from north-east to south. The account is a complicated one, but may be summarized by saying that the migration was part of a general movement of a pre-Nyika and pre-Kamba group of peoples from the north of the Tana River near the coast which began about five centuries ago and continued in the coast area about two centuries ago. Lambert estimates that the movement reached Fort Hall about A.D. 1550, and Kiambu about A.D. 1800.[24] The movement across the Chania River into Kiambu was still going on at the time of the British

[19] The fullest account of the traditions of these peoples is that of Lambert, 1950, pp. 12 ff.; see also Gurney, 1929, pp. 203–4; Shackleton, 1930, pp. 201–2; Bernardi, 1959, p. 6.

[20] Fullest account is in Lambert, 1950, pp. 44 ff., 79 ff.; also Kenyatta, 1938, pp. 23–4; Routledge, 1910, pp. 3–4; Maxwell Report, 1929, p. 6; Stannus, 1915, p. 131; Cagnolo, 1933, p. 19; Boyes, 1911, p. 297; Bernardi, 1959, p. 6; K. R. Dundas states that the Kikuyu term refers to the Aathi or Dorobo.

[21] The evidence is considered at length by Lambert, 1950, pp. 48 ff.

[22] The historical and ethnological evidence is discussed at length by Lambert, 1950, pp. 54 ff. For detailed material on the Dorobo, see Schapera, 1949, p. 14. The best accounts of the modern Dorobo are by Huntingford (1951, 1954, 1955). For their relationship with the Kikuyu in particular, see, besides Lambert, Routledge, 1910, p. 5; K. R. Dundas, 1, 1908, pp. 136–8; Cagnolo, 1933, p. 19; Hobley, 1910, pp. 131–6; Phillips, 1945, p. 60; Maxwell Report, 1929, pp. 6–7; K.L.C. Evidence, 1932, I, *passim*.

[23] See Lambert, 1950, *passim*, and below, pp. 48–9.

[24] Lambert, 1950, pp. 27 ff. See also Huntingford 1963, p. 90.

occupation of South Kikuyu, and Routledge states that in the north groups were still advancing westwards at the rate of ten to fifteen miles a year within the memory of his informants.[25]

The Kikuyu have various myths of origin which reflect their relations with other peoples. One tells that the three sons of Mumbere, the creator of the world, Masai, Gikuyu and Kamba, were given a choice by their father of a spear, bow, and digging-stick: Masai chose the spear, Kamba the bow, and Gikuyu the digging-stick. A similar myth says that the three sons were Masai, Gikuyu and Dorobo; the Masai were told to hold the plains and keep livestock, Gikuyu was told to live by agriculture, and Dorobo to hunt game. There are myths of the same sort among the Meru tribes.[26]

The Kikuyu say they are descendants of Gikuyu and his wife Muumbi ("the creator"), who lived at Mukurue wa Gathanga, near the present Fort Hall. Muumbi gave birth to nine daughters, from whom are descended the nine Kikuyu clans.[27] The Meru have a tradition of coming from a place to the east called Mbwa, which they left some two hundred years ago; the period can be estimated from a study of generation-sets. They found the Mwoko in occupation of their present home, and absorbed some and drove out others.[28]

The Chuka are regarded as being the only indigenous tribe in the Northern area. They are distinct in physical characteristics, in certain cultural features, such as the use of shield-sticks and stone-headed clubs (both these weapons also being used by the Mwimbi but by no other group of this cluster).[29] In the middle of the last century the Chuka were invaded by the Meru and Mwimbi; the Mwimbi settled, with quantities of Chuka livestock and women. The area so settled is now known as Muthambi.[30] The Mwimbi and the Chuka have no tradition of immigration from another place.[31]

The Tharaka claim to have come from the east across the River Tana. Today they are a culturally distinct tribe in many ways, which may partly at least be explained by their geographical isolation in the low-lying area near the Tana Valley.[32] They may be of Pokomo origin. They are like the Kamba but unlike all other Kikuyu tribes in having no system of generation-sets.[33]

Modern Developments

The Kikuyu have been noted as a people who quickly adapted themselves to changing situations; they are today one of the leading groups in the East Africa political field.

The first European to enter Kikuyu seems to have been the missionary Krapf, who reached the Tana River in 1848–9. In 1883 Fischer crossed Kikuyu, fighting all the way, and Thomson skirted the country in 1885, but their accounts are unhelpful.[34] In 1887 Teleki and von Höhnel traversed Kikuyu from south to north: their account is most valuable.[35] After that date many travellers entered the country.

[25] Routledge, 1910, p. 7; see also Tate, 1910, p. 236; Hobley, 1910, p. 135; C. Dundas, 1915, p. 245; K. R. Dundas I, 1908, p. 137; Hobley and K. R. Dundas give origins of certain supposedly foreign clans.

[26] Lambert, 1950, pp. 16 ff.; Routledge, 1910, p. 283; Kenyatta, 1938, p. 3; Tate, 1910, p. 236; K. R. Dundas, 1, 1908, p. 139.

[27] Kenyatta, 1938, pp. 4, 23; Lambert, 1950, pp. 19 ff.; Beecher, 1938, pp. 18–2.

[28] Mbwa may have etymological connection with the Swahili *pwa-ni Coast* (lit., at the coast). See Lambert, 1950, pp. 7 ff.; Bernardi, 1959, p. 52 ff.; Laughton, 1944, p. 2; Holding, 1942, pp. 58–9; K.L.C. Evidence, 1932, I, p. 559; Hobley 1910, p. 156; Gurney, 1929, pp. 203–4.

[29] Orde-Browne, 1925, pp. 20, 42–4; 1916, pp. 229–30; Lambert, 1950, pp. 14, 17, 73.

[30] Orde-Browne, 1925, pp. 25–6, 32–3; 1916, p. 226; Gurney, 1929, p. 204; Lambert, 1950, pp. 14, 17, 75.

[31] Lambert, 1950, p. 14.

[32] Lambert, 1950, p. 15; Champion, 1912, pp. 69–70; Hobley, 1910, p. 2; but see Prins, 1952, p. 3.

[37] See below, p. 37.

[34] See Bibliography.

[35] Von Höhnel, 1894.

In 1888 the Imperial British East Africa Company was given a royal charter, and in 1890 Lugard left Mombasa to build a caravan station at Ngong Bagas; he found the site unsuitable and built a station at Dagoretti in Kiambu. It was destroyed in 1891, and in the same year Fort Smith was built as a government station. Fort Smith is near the site of the present-day Kabete. Fort Hall was built in 1901. The Embu Expedition in 1906 resulted in the building of Meru Station in 1908, followed by Chuka Station in 1913.[36]

Missions working in Kikuyu are:[37]

Protestant: Church Missionary Society, Church of Scotland Mission, Methodist Missionary Society, Africa Inland Mission, Gospel Missionary Society and Salvation Army.

Catholic: Mission of the Consolata and the Holy Ghost Mission.

There are schools, both primary and secondary, staffed in agreement with various missions, and there are also many independent schools of the Kikuyu Independent Schools Associations.

From the beginning of the century onwards the Kikuyu were excluded from certain areas, particularly in the south, which were alienated to European farmers. Of a total of 1,800 square miles, 109·5 square miles were alienated, which included much valuable coffee-growing land near Nairobi.[38] In 1948 there were many thousand Kikuyu "squatters" working on European farms and a very large number working in Nairobi.[39] In south Kiambu the indigenous tribal social organization has changed to a very considerable extent. Kikuyu has been marked by a history of political movements and associations, since the formation of the Kikuyu Association in 1920. The history of the growth of the various associations and trades unions cannot be given here: the best known have included the Kenya African Union, the Kikuyu Central Association (founded in 1925), the Kikuyu Independent Schools Association and the Kikuyu Karinga Educational Association. These were all closely linked with religious movements, which are mentioned on page 64 below.[40]

LANGUAGE

All the Kikuyu speak closely related Bantu languages. Doke classifies them as falling within the "northern Zone" of Bantu, which includes Gishu, Nyoro, Ganda, etc., and Guthrie places them in his "Zone E, group 50". According to Lambert, the Kikuyu languages can be divided into two groups: one includes Kikuyu, Ndia, Kichugu, Embu, Mbere, and is closely related to Kamba; the other includes Meru, Muthambi and Mwimbi, and shows close affinity with the coast languages Pokomo and Nyika. He adds that Chuka and Tharaka fall between the two groups.[41]

Phonetic and grammatical characteristics are given by Doke, Guthrie and Lambert,[42] and a list of grammars, vocabularies and other works on Kikuyu languages are given by Whiteley and Gutkind and Doke.[43]

The *lingua franca* in use between Kikuyu and Europeans or Indians has until recently been a form of Swahili, the language of the coast of East Africa.[44] English is also widely spoken today.

PHYSICAL ENVIRONMENT

The most useful general account is given in the East African Royal Commission Report of 1955.[45] Kikuyu has two rainy seasons annually: the long rains from

[36] For early history of the I.B.E.A. Company, see MacDonald, 1897, p. 111; Tate, 1910, p. 233; Hall, 1938, *passim*; Orde-Browne, 1925, p. 34.

[37] Philp, 1936, gives history and statistical data for missions.

[38] Kenya Land Commission Report, Ch. VI.

[39] See Demographic data, p. 12.

[40] The most concise account of these political movements is in Middleton, 1965, which contains references to the main sources.

[41] Doke, 1945, pp. 9, 10, 14; Lambert, 1950, pp. 4 ff.; Guthrie, 1948, pp. 43–5.

[42] Doke, 1945, and Guthrie, 1948; Lambert, 1950, p. 5.

[43] Whiteley and Gutkind, 1958; Doke, 1945, pp. 14–15.

[44] See Doke, 1945, pp. 56–66, especially p. 64.

[45] Great Britain, *East African Royal Commission Report*, 1955, p. 8–9.

April to June, and the short rains in November and December. The rainfall is heavy and there are many permanent rivers, almost all of which flow eastwards into the Tana (Thagana) and Athi Rivers, which flow across Kamba country into the Indian Ocean. They almost all rise on either Mount Kenya or the Aberdare Range.

Routledge wrote of the country that it "consists of a sea of ridge-like hills. . . . These hills and ridges are from 200 to 600 feet high, divided by well-watered valleys, and a traveller standing on the higher levels of the Aberdare Range and looking towards (Mount) Kenya is reminded of the waves of a heavy cross sea."[46] The ridges and rivers run in a general north-west to south-east direction.

Kikuyu is a land of great natural fertility, although soil deterioration has caused serious problems. The soil is usually deep and rich, derived from soft volcanic tuffs that supported dense forest down to the time of the incoming of the Kikuyu. It is retentive of moisture on account of its fine-grained texture, and remains moist even in time of drought: it is also light to work.[47]

A good account of the flora and fauna of Kikuyu proper is given by Crawshay, and of Embu and Meru by Orde-Browne.[48]

Before the Kikuyu spread over their present lands the area was densely forested, but today almost the only forest left is an almost continuous fringe, eight to fifteen miles in width, on the lower slopes of Mount Kenya. The Embu, Chuka, Mwimbi and Meru live in this forest belt on the eastern slopes of the mountain and on the adjoining Nyombeni Range. Most of the country of the Kikuyu proper has largely been deforested.[49] This deforestation was in an advanced stage when the first Europeans entered the region except for the belt of forest left on the marches of the country.[50] In recent years there has been much reforestation carried out under governmental auspices.

MAIN FEATURES OF ECONOMY

Agriculture, Livestock and Diet

In the past the main crops of the Kikuyu were *sorghum vulgare*, various millets, beans and sweet potatoes. Today maize is the most important crop, both for subsistence and for sale. Other crops grown are pigeon pea, European potatoes, manioc (cassava), bananas, sugar-cane, yams, arum lily and various fruits. In addition, tobacco, coffee and the castor-oil tree (the oil of which is used as a toilet grease) are grown. Most of these except coffee were grown when von Höhnel visited Kikuyu: he states that millets, beans and potatoes were most plentiful in the South, while bananas were commonest in the north; millet was not grown in the north. Today coffee, tea and pyrethrum are grown, largely for export.[51]

Among the Northern tribes the staple crops were, and to a great extent still are, millets and black and tree beans. Supplementary foods are maize, yams, bananas, sweet potatoes, manioc, sugar-cane and many kinds of peas and beans. Important cash crops are maize and coffee.[52]

Tobacco is casually cultivated, and when dried is made up for sale into a rope; it is then ground down with a little fat. Tobacco and snuff are used mostly by the older people only, although young men may take snuff.[53]

[46] Routledge, 1910, pp. 2, 40; von Höhnel, 1894, I, p. 351; Crawshay, 1902, p. 27; Dickson, 1903, p. 36; Cagnolo, 1933, pp. 7–8, 195–6; Fitzgerald, 1950, p. 253.

[47] Fitzgerald, 1950; Humphrey, 1945, *passim*.

[48] Crawshay, 1902, pp. 45–9; Orde-Browne, 1925, pp. 237–57.

[49] Fitzgerald, 1950; Routledge, 1910, p. 2; von Höhnel, 1894, I, p. 351; Stigand, 1913, p. 235.

[50] Von Höhnel, 1894, I, pp. 302, 352; also Stigand, 1913, p. 236; Mackinder, 1900, p. 461; Arkell-Hardwick, 1903, pp. 70, 91; Patterson, 1909, p. 339; Lugard, 1893, p. 328.

[51] Routledge, 1910, pp. 42–3, 53, 54, 56, 65; K.L.C. Evidence, 1932, I, p. 976; Humphrey, 1945, p. 20; Kenyatta, 1938, p. 58: Cagnolo, 1933, pp. 8–10; Tate, I, 1904, p. 132; 2, 1904, pp. 258–9; Crawshay, 1902, p. 26; von Höhnel, 1894, I, pp. 352–3; Stigand, 1913, p. 238; Arkell-Hardwick, 1903, pp. 52–3; Boyes, 1911, pp. 267, 301–2.

[52] Laughton, 1944, pp. 5–7; Champion, 1912, p. 80; Orde-Browne, 1925, p. 98; Lambert, 1947, p. 3; Gurney, 1929, p. 206.

[53] Routledge 1910, pp. 24–5; Champion, 1912, p. 90; Orde-Browne, 1925, p. 129.

There are two crop cycles in a year of twelve months.[54] Planting follows the beginning of the rains, and harvesting takes place as soon as the crop is ripe after the end of the rains, usually in the sixth month.

Traditionally manure was not used. MacDonald and Lugard mention the digging of irrigation channels,[55] and the Northern tribes practised indigenous methods of soil conservation. The Chuka terraced hillsides with wattle or stone barriers, and the Meru made box terraces with garden trash, and also planted live wash-stops on steep slopes.[56]

The Kikuyu diet was mainly vegetarian. The diets of men and women differed considerably, the women eating no meat but eating several kinds of vegetables not used by men. The Kikuyu ate game only rarely and eggs and fish not at all; fish-eating caused ritual uncleanness. Among the Tharaka only uncircumcised persons ate wild birds and fowls, eggs were eaten by no one, but meat and animal game by everybody. The Chuka ate all meat except fowl; the Mwimbi, Embu and Mbere ate certain kinds of game. None of the Northern tribes ate fish or eggs.[57]

Various methods of cooking vegetables and meat were in use.[58] The favourite animal for slaughter was a full-grown castrated ram kept in the dark of the hut for three months and fed on sweet potato tops. Cattle and goats were eaten when they died a natural death, or at times of famine, and at sacrifices.[59]

The Kikuyu kept many goats and sheep, and also cattle. The standard value of commodities was traditionally reckoned in goats, although cattle had great prestige value (the owner of many cattle was given praise-names in songs). Any man of standing owned 10 or 12 head of cattle, and a considerable number of goats and sheep. Only men and boys might handle cattle.[60]

The consumption of cows' milk was small. Among the Northern tribes a gap of three months was left between eating meat and drinking milk. Goats' milk was drunk by women and children only among the Kikuyu, but not at all by the Northern tribes. The blood of cattle, taken from the jugular vein by an arrow, was drunk by warriors, a custom apparently copied from the Masai.[61]

Honey was collected by all tribes and beer was made from honey and sugar-cane; the Northern tribes also made a beer from millet. Among the Kikuyu beer could properly be drunk only by the old, although it was frequently also drunk by warriors; among the Mwimbi it was drunk by women and children also.[62]

There are no salt deposits in Kikuyu. Salt was obtained by external trade, or in the form of ash from papyrus burning. Livestock were taken to deposits of saline clay, which was also made into cakes and placed in the goats' trough in the homestead. This saline earth was also occasionally eaten by human beings.[63]

The diet of the present day Kikuyu still contains most of the foods mentioned, maize, beans, sweet and European potatoes, bananas and vegetables. The modern

[54] See Kenyatta, 1938, pp. 57–9; K. R. Dundas, 1909, p. 38, and Routledge, 1910, pp. 40–1, for details of the agricultural calendar.

[55] MacDonald, 1897, p. 109; Lugard, 1893, p. 328.

[56] Orde-Browne, 1916, pp. 227–8; Laughton, 1944, p. 7.

[57] Orr and Gilks, 1931, pp. 21, 26–7; a chemical analysis of Kikuyu diet is given on pp. 22 ff. and 67 ff.; Routledge, 1910, p. 49; Kenyatta, 1938, pp. 64–5, 207; Cagnolo, 1933, p. 118; Anderson, 1937, *passim*; Orde-Browne, 1916 p. 227; 1925, pp. 98–9.

[58] For details see Routledge, 1910, pp. 50–5; Tate, 2, 1904, pp. 259–60; Orde-Browne, 1925, pp. 101–2.

[59] Routledge, 1910, p. 50; Kenyatta, 1938, p. 64.

[60] Kenyatta, 1938, pp. xv, 65; Tate, 1, 1904, p. 132; Stigand, 1913, p. 237; Orde-Browne, 1925, p. 117, and 1916, p. 227; Laughton, 1944, p. 5; Routledge, 1910, pp. 45–6; Champion, 1912, p. 69; see Kenyatta, 1938, pp. 66–7, and Leakey, 3, 1934, for a discussion of the value of goats in Kikuyu life.

[61] Kenyatta, 1938, p. 64; Orr and Gilks, 1931, p. 21; Routledge, 1910, pp. 46, 47, 174–5; Orde-Browne, 1925, pp. 100, 119; Stigand, 1913, pp. 241–2.

[62] Routledge, 1910, pp. 56–7, 61–4; Stigand, 1913, p. 239. Both these writers give details of making honey beer. See also Orde-Browne, 1925, pp. 104–9; von Höhnel, 1894, pp. 352–3; Boyes, 1911, p. 267; Crawshay, 1902, p. 42; Champion, 1912, p. 81; Gurney, 1929, p. 206.

[63] Routledge, 1910, p. 58; Orr and Gilks 1931, p. 21; Orde-Browne, 1925, p. 104; Boyes, 1911, pp. 129–30.

additions, bread, tea, milk (especially tea), and rice are of growing importance, as is meat. Individual diets vary with wealth, availability of land to grow food, and place of living.

The use of manure and fertilizer has increased both the productivity of the land and the variety of crops. Vegetables are widely grown; whether they have a place in the daily diet depends on such factors as easy access to a market and the degree of wealth of the owners as well as on personal preference. The same is true for poultry and eggs.

TRADE

There has always been considerable internal trade among the Kikuyu; large markets have been, and are, an important feature of Kikuyu life, except among the Northern tribes.

Markets are held in any open space chosen in accordance with the convenience of a scattered population, and in more populous districts are frequently not more than seven miles apart. Traditionally a market is usually held on such a site every fourth day, and the dates are arranged so as not to clash with similar functions in the neighbourhood. Feuds and fighting stopped on market days, and the markets were "policed" by members of the warrior grade.[64]

At the time Routledge was writing, almost all exchange was still by barter, although beads were used as currency. Since then the use of money has become almost universal.[65]

The commodities traded in markets included iron and iron objects, salt and salt-earths, ochre, pottery and other goods whose production was in the hands of specialists. However, commodities produced by non-specialists were also exchanged: they included tobacco, fat, string, beer and foodstuffs. Today trade includes a wide range of imported consumer goods.

Spears and swords, tobacco, gourds, honey and ochre were traded with the Masai for livestock; they were not traded at fixed markets but were taken into Masailand by a group of men who would form a "trading guild": protection was given by alliance with a "friend who acted as the guide and protector of his friends and their goods". Trading was also done by women, who could pass with immunity into the other tribe's territory, apparently even when warfare was taking place.[66]

Exchange between the Kikuyu and Kamba depended on seasonal harvests, since the two tribes produce much the same goods. Besides foodstuffs in times of shortage, which were exchanged for livestock and sometimes ivory, objects exchanged included chains, snuff-boxes, bows and arrows, and medicines.[67]

There was some trade between the Tharaka and Kamba, the former exchanging foodstuffs for beads and wire. The Mbere, who are great bee-keepers, traded in honey and beeswax.[68]

The southern Kikuyu had contact with the Arab and European ivory traders who flourished during the last century. The main route for this traffic in Kenya—the "Uganda road" from the coast to Lake Victoria, which was used in spite of the Masai and became additionally important when the English were opening up the country at the end of the last century—just touched Kikuyuland in the south. At that point were established several trading posts (Dagoretti, Fort Smith, Kikuyu Station) which were used as resting and revictualling stations for the caravans. The early traders did not interfere with the Kikuyu: it was more politic to maintain friendly relations so as to be able to acquire grain.[69] The Kikuyu sold great quantities of vegetable

[64] Orde-Browne, 1925, p. 116; Routledge, 1910, p. 105; see also Cagnolo, 1933, pp. 42, 44, 194; K. R. Dundas, 1909, p. 38; Boyes, 1911, p. 92; von Höhnel, 1894, I, p. 293.

[65] Routledge, 1910, p. 106; Cagnolo, 1933, p. 43; but see Kenyatta, 1938, p. 61, who says that barter was still the commonest form of exchange in 1938.

[66] Kenyatta, 1938, p. 68; Stigand, 1913, p. 241; Thomson, 1885, p. 178; von Höhnel, 1894, I, p. 291; MacDonald, 1897, p. 110.

[67] Kenyatta, 1938, p. 69.

[68] Champion, 1912, p. 69; Orde-Browne, 1925, p. 107.

[69] Routledge, 1910, pp. 15–16; von Höhnel, 1894, I, pp. 286–9; Thomson, 1885, p. 307; Guillain, 1853, p. 289; Lugard, 1893, p. 328.

produce and livestock to the caravans; von Höhnel states that the commodities preferred in exchange for grain were Masai beads and brass wire. The Masai acquired trade wire, salt, etc., as "tribute" from caravans, and some of these articles filtered through to the Kikuyu.[70] The Kikuyu also traded ivory, which they obtained from the Dorobo in the forests.[71]

In recent years the Kikuyu economy has been based largely upon cash crop farming. Until the second world war the Kikuyu were debarred from taking part in the growing of coffee. Since these restrictions were lifted a rapidly growing number of farmers have engaged in growing coffee, pyrethrum, tea, and other crops. Strong co-operatives have their own nurseries, advise in planting and organize the sale of the products. Land consolidation with a consequent security of tenure has given impetus to improvement of the land and loans can now be obtained by farmers. This has resulted in increased investment and the production of cash crops able to compete in the world market. An extensive trade in vegetables, poultry and eggs had developed before the Emergency and is gaining in importance. The introduction of high grade cattle and the breeding of beasts both for meat and milk is a growing concern of a number of larger farms. The expansion of the growing of cash crops is to a large extent dependent on the need for finding markets, both internal and external and on a good internal road system for the remoter parts of the country.[72]

Forms of Economic Organization

Among the Kikuyu land was held by the joint family—*mbari*—and plots were allocated by the head; among the Northern tribes the land-holding unit was a kin-group of wider span. Each domestic family (elementary or polygynous) was a basic economic unit, producing and consuming its own food, within the framework of the wider land-holding group.[73] Each "house" (the hut of one wife) had its own goats, implements and furniture, which were under the control of the wife and transmitted to her sons at her death.[74]

There was a good deal of co-operative work within the joint family. The members of a family-group would plant all their cereals in one block, though each "house" would retain individual ownership in a particular piece. Bird-scaring and night-watching could thus be equitably shared amongst the group. It was a recognized custom—*ngwatio*—for the women to cultivate the fields as a group, but each woman's plot was demarcated by pigeon pea or sorghum, so that at harvest time each would gather in her individual share. Work-parties functioned in the building of houses, in breaking new land and in work amongst the sugar-cane. These practices resulted in the land of a *githaka*[75] becoming roughly divided up into areas each earmarked for sharing amongst all for the special purpose for which it was considered suitable.[76]

Distribution of Labour

The traditional sexual division of labour was similar among both the Kikuyu and the Northern tribes, although the material on the latter is very scanty.[77]

Men[78] were responsible for:

(a) Tending of cattle, in all its aspects, and trading in livestock;

[70] Von Höhnel, 1894, pp. 297, 315; Routledge, 1910, p. 16.

[71] Wakefield, 1870.

[72] Gourou 1954, Hughes 1955, Pedraza 1956, Kolbe and Fouche 1959, Penwill 1960, and annual reports of the Kenya Department of Agriculture.

[73] See section on Land Tenure, below; Kenyatta, 1938, pp. 53–5.

[74] Routledge, 1910, pp. 47, 12; Kenyatta, 1938, pp. 10, 63, 177–8; see section on Inheritance, below, pp. 46–7.

[75] The land held by a joint family or segment of a joint family.

[76] Humphrey, 1945, pp. 20, 22; see also Kenyatta, 1938, pp. 59–60, 78, 94; Cagnolo, 1933, p. 53; Routledge, 1910, p. 41.

[77] C. Dundas, 1915, pp. 301–2; Champion, 1912, p. 80.

[78] Routledge, 1910, pp. 39, 45, 78, 121; Kenyatta, 1938, pp. 53–7, 63, 90–4; C. Dundas, 1915; Hobley, 1938, pp. 278–9; Cagnolo, 1933; Tate, 1, 1904, p. 133.

(b) Clearing the fields, breaking up the surface for the women, cutting drains and water-furrows, building roads and bridges (men might cultivate fields if for any reason the women could not: it was not considered derogatory);
(c) Planting certain crops: bananas, yams, sweet potatoes, sugar-cane and tobacco;
(d) Scaring birds; pruning bananas, cutting and bringing home sugar-cane for beer, and straining the juice;
(e) Uprooting the grain stalks after harvest and burning them to fertilize the ground and kill pests;
(f) Collecting honey;
(g) Hunting and fighting;
(h) Cutting and erecting timbers in house-building; building fences and granaries;
(i) Making wooden utensils; mending cracked calabashes; working in ivory and iron; tanning leather and making clothes of skins; making the string used in beer-making and hunting, and binding the sweet potato tops which are given to the ram kept for fattening in the hut;
(j) Legal and ritual duties.

Women,[79] in addition to taking care of children, were responsible for:
(a) planting maize, millet, beans and other crops, hoeing and weeding, harvesting crops;
(b) Storing and caring for the food supply, cooking; fetching water and fire-wood, grinding grain and pounding sugar-cane for beer; tending hives and making honey;
(c) Thatching and plastering in hut-building;
(d) Sewing skins; making pottery; collecting iron ore; making string required for making baskets for tying leaves used at initiation ceremony; making baskets and bead-work;
(e) Trading in grain;
(f) Certain ritual duties, depending on the social status of her husband.

CRAFTS

The raw materials available for the indigenous productive system of the Kikuyu tribes were wood, iron, clay, animal products and plant products, all of which were found within Kikuyu itself.

(*a*) *Hut-building*.[80] The traditional circular Kikuyu hut has walls made of wooden poles, filled in with wattle-sticks and daubed with clay, or of trimmed planks set edge to edge. The framework for the conical roof is made separately, lifted on to the walls, and then thatched. The eaves are supported by poles set outside the walls. The huts of the Northern tribes resemble those of the Kikuyu in appearance and method of construction, but are usually smaller and of poorer workmanship, especially in Chuka. A well-built hut generally lasts ten or more years, with occasional re-thatching.

Traditionally for a new hut the three stones which formed the fireplace must be "new and uncontaminated", and fire must be drilled from fire-sticks; but if an old hut was being rebuilt it is sufficient for fire to be brought from the old hut. If the fire in a hut goes out, ritual purification is generally carried out for the inmates, although it does not make them ritually unclean.

Each hut has its granary, a large basket set on wooden legs, and shaped like a small hut.

[79] Routledge, 1910, pp. 39, 59, 78, 81, 98, 121–3; Kenyatta, 1938, pp. 54–5, 63, 87–9; Hobley, 1938, pp. 238, 277–9; C. Dundas, 1915, p. 301; Orde-Browne, 1925, p. 100; Cagnolo, 1933, p. 55.

[80] There are several good and illustrated accounts, the best being Routledge, 1910, pp. 66–71; see also Routledge, pp. 77, 118; Kenyatta, 1938, pp. 76–84; Cagnolo, 1933, pp. 33, 53–7; Boyes, 1911, p. 83; von Höhnel, 1894, I, p. 318; Stigand, 1913, p. 235; Crawshay, 1902, pp. 33–4; Orde-Brown, 1916, p. 228; 1925, pp. 103, 110–16; Champion, 1912, p. 74.

(*b*) *Agricultural implements.*[81] The Kikuyu have two principal agricultural implements, a seven-foot wooden stake (Routledge's "crowbar") and an iron-tipped digging-stick; the Meru use a wooden digging-stick. Other tools used include the knife and axe. Today the imported iron *panga*—a heavy one-edged knife—is widely used.

(*c*) *Traps*. The Northern tribes make considerable use of animal and bird traps.

(*d*) *Weapons*. The Kikuyu weapons consist of bows and arrows, throwing-clubs (Routledge's "life-preserver"), spear, sword, shield and sling. The Northern tribes have similar weapons, though slightly different in shape. The Chuka make a double-ended spear, and Chuka and Embu use stone-headed clubs and shield-sticks (the latter being used only in dances).

(*e*) *Milking vessels, etc*. Calabashes and gourds are used for milking, and for cooking and household vessels.

(*f*) *Wooden implements*. Besides agricultural implements and weapons made of wood, wood is also used for bee-boxes, household furniture, wooden mortars, the stools carried by old men, and pipes.

(*g*) *Pottery*. Pottery is made by women specialists, men being debarred from any contact with the process. The only products are two types of pot, one wide-mouthed, the other narrow-mouthed, and the nozzles for the smiths' bellows, made in two sizes.

Among the Kikuyu the top half of the pot is made first by building up from a coil of clay; this half is then turned upside down and the base completed; the pot is then fired. Among the Northern tribes the two halves are made separately and joined.

(*h*) *String-, basket- and mat-making*. String is made from bark and animal tendons by both men and women, according to the use to which it is to be put. Baskets are made of string, by women only, but men are not debarred from contact with any part of the process. Grass mats are made by the Northern tribes.

(*i*) *Tanning*. Skins are tanned by men for the making of clothes, shields, quivers, etc.

(*j*) *Bridge-building*. The Kikuyu are experts at building suspension bridges, using various creepers.

(*k*) *Fire-making*. The indigenous method of making fire is by the use of the hand-drill. The "female" fire-stick must be made of the wood of the *mugumu* or sacred fig-tree.

(*l*) *Iron-making*. Iron is used for making implements and weapons already listed, and for chains, wire, and other objects. The ore is obtained from open sites; in Kikuyu it is collected by women and children in the "quarries", and in Tharaka it is found in the form of magnetite deposited in river beds after heavy rain. The washing of the ore is done by both sexes, but the smelting is done by men only.

Tools used for smelting and forging are granite anvils, tongs, furnace and bellows; the Kikuyu hammer is of a curious type.

Smiths are supposed to have come from the north-west of Mount Kenya; they are now scattered throughout Kikuyu, among all clans. Although certain families are all smiths, a smith must be initiated into the craft, and the son of a smith cannot practise until so initiated.[82]

[81] For references to and illustrations of (*b*) to (*l*) above, see: Routledge, 1910, pp. 16, 40, 46, 56–8, 71, 97, 102; Kenyatta, 1938, pp. 72–5, 85–7, 89–92; Cagnolo, 1933, pp. 32, 37–41, 226–8; Orde-Browne, 1916, pp. 228–9; 1925, pp. 118, 120–3, 129–33, 143–50, 165–6; von Höhnel, 1894, I, p. 356; Boyes, 1911, p. 89; Hobley, 1938, pp. 167–9; Laughton, 1944, pp. 8, 16; Crawshay, 1902, pp. 29, 34; Bugeau, 1943, p. 205; Arkell-Hardwick, 1903, p. 238; Thomson, 1885, p. 177; Champion, 1912, pp. 70–1, 77–80, 90; Eliot, 1905, p. 128; Tate, 2, 1904, pp. 257–8; Beech, 1913, pp. 4; Lindblom, 1920, p. 532.

[82] See below, pp. 66–7, for description of smiths' magical powers.

Arts, Music, Dances and Games[83]

Initiation shields are painted with coloured designs; there are apparently no conventional patterns associated with clans or other groupings, the designs depending on individual choice. Some are said to be copied from those of the Masai. In some parts of Kikuyu bee-boxes are decorated. Kikuyu boys sometimes have picture-rattles which are gourds decorated with cowrie shells and coloured lines representing a story. Routledge was told that the art of making them had been forgotten.

Children make unburnt clay models of animals, etc., and Routledge mentions anthropomorphic clay figures used in ritual dances.

Kikuyu musical instruments consist of single-membrane drums (apparently of foreign origin), flutes, whistles, side-blown horns, rattles and bells. Flutes and whistles are played by men only, and it is taboo to play them inside a hut. No mention is made of specialists except by Boyes, who writes of itinerant minstrels who were privileged to travel safely throughout the country.

The Kikuyu have many dances, which may be distinguished by the age and sex of the dancers; for example, those danced by uninitiated boys, by warriors, by women only and by men and women together.

There are various initiative and physical games, including games with miniature weapons; a board game similar to the Swahili *mbau* is common. There are many riddles and series of questions and answers which must be learnt by rote.

KIKUYU SOCIAL AND POLITICAL INSTITUTIONS

Social and political relationships among the Kikuyu proper are organised in two main categories: groups based on ties of land and marriage and groups cutting across these specific ties, based on status, age and generation within a given territory.

The first group comprises the *muhiriga* (pl. *mihiriga*), translated by "clans" in most of the literature and the *mbari*, "lineages", the second the age or status grades, the age-sets and the generation set system, the latter two called *rika* (pl. *marika*). The territorial units within which they operate are the *ituura* (dwelling-place), the *rugongo* (ridge) and the *bururi* (used alternatively for a district or for the whole of Kikuyu country).

The Mihiriga

One of the Kikuyu myths of origin is also a myth concerning the origin of the *mihiriga*. The ancestral couple Gikuyu and Muumbi had been given land by Ngai (the deity). They had nine daughters, but no sons. One day they were visited by nine men who were so pleased with the daughters that they stayed and married them. The legend does not mention the payment of *ruracio* or bridewealth. The nine daughters' offspring were thus the offspring of Gikuyu and Muumbi and all Kikuyu are children of Gikuyu and Muumbi with mythical rights within the ancestral territory. The nine daughters gave their names to the principal Kikuyu *mihiriga*.

The *muhiriga* is a mythically validated descent group with members having mythically validated rights within the ancestral land.

Lists of clan names are given by several writers, and vary from nine to thirteen.[84] The lists given by Kenyatta, Hobley and the Maxwell Report agree, there being variant names for some of the clans.[85] The clans are patrilineal and in the early

[83] For descriptions and illustrations, see Routledge, 1910, pp. 108–15, 178–92, 350–2; also 1906; Hobley, 1910, p. 132; 1, 1911, pp. 439–56; 1938, pp. 266–73; Joyce, 1906; Orde-Browne, 1925, pp. 125–8, 141, 164–72, 221–5; Cagnolo, 1933, pp. 76, 165–72, 189, 247–9; Kenyatta, 1938, pp. 93–7, 101, 104; Boyes, 1911, p. 104; Bugeau, 1943, pp. 192–4. Dances of the Northern tribes: Orde-Browne, 1925, pp. 173–80; Champion, 1912, pp. 82–3; Gurney, 1929, p. 205.

[84] Kenyatta, 1938, pp. 5–6 (nine clans plus "others which are more or less variations of the original ones"); Hobley, 1906, p. 83 (nine clans); Maxwell Report, Appendix, 1929, p. 46 (nine clans); Cagnolo, 1933, p. 21 (ten clans); Tate, 1910, p. 237 (eleven clans); Routledge, 1910, p. 21 (thirteen clans).

[85] The names are Aceera or Anjeeri, Anjiru, Agaciku, Angui or Aithiageni, Ambui, Aithaga or Akiuru or Ambura, Angari or Aithikahunu, Aithirandu or Angeci, Agathigia or Airimu or Aicakamuyu.

literature said to be totemic.[86] They are dispersed across Kikuyu, although Hobley states that "until recently" they were associated with particular places.[87] Routledge states that they are exogamous, but as a general statement this is incorrect. Within clans are smaller units, the *mbari*, and these, or a group of these, are exogamous units.[88]

There seem to be certain links between clans; Routledge states that there are said to be certain restrictions as to marriage between particular clans.[89] K. R. Dundas states that some of the Kikuyu clans are the same as some of the Masai clans, and some are linked with Kamba clans bearing the same names[90] Tate states that five of the Kikuyu clans are regarded as being more powerful than the remainder and did not pay blood-money for the killing of a member of a "minor" clan, but the Maxwell Report states specifically that they are all of equal status. Tate adds that these five senior clans have "chiefs" and Routledge states that "some clans have recognized headmen".[91]

There is no specific information about the internal composition of the clan except that it is divided into sub-clans, which are in turn sub-divided, the smallest named segment being the *mbari*. In the early literature confusion arises from the fact that writers attribute to "the clan" behaviour which is in fact attributable to a *mbari* or group of *mbari* only.

The clan is said to be the unit which admits mutual responsibility for homicide and compensation[92] but this means that *de facto* some kin-grouping within the clan will be responsible, and not necessarily the whole clan, which will be widely dispersed, and which may be of a very large size. Routledge says that the chief bond of solidarity is mutual responsibility for the murder fine, which can be collected from all members of the clan over a very large district: the actual span of the group concerned is uncertain. Dundas states that only a "near relative" of a murderer could be killed in blood-vengeance. It seems from Routledge's account that the group concerned is of fairly wide span; from Dundas's statement it might be quite small. Authorities agree that the group concerned in feuds is the *mbari* or *ituura*.[93]

The district is the unit for initiation ceremonies, but the clan is significant at these ceremonies, which vary according to clan. Clearly, no clan is contained in any one district, so that for this ceremony a clan is split up into many segments; similarly, a district must be split up into many sections belonging to different clans, each with its own form of rites. According to the Maxwell Report, the test of whether clan segments have remained "united" is whether they continue to take part in common initiation ceremonies, family and "group" sacrifices, contribution to blood-money, eating of sacrificial animals in marriage transactions, and family ceremonial eating of meat. Hobley adds that clan members "in the neighbourhood" attend wedding feasts, and assemble at a man's death. In Nyeri the "clan elders" come together for ritual purposes and in Fort Hall the "elders of the sub-clan and some of the main clan" take part in land transactions.[94]

It is impossible to say definitely that there are descent-groups of any certain size which operate in specific situations, but it seems that clan meetings take place

[86] Routledge, 1910, p. 20; Cagnolo, 1933, p. 22, states that they are totemic or "semi-totemic"; Hobley, 1906, p. 83, gives a list of totems. Routledge quotes a missionary who considered that "totems exist in particular families but that the same totems would not obtain throughout a whole clan" (p. 22).

[87] Routledge, 1910, pp. 20, 196; Maxwell Report, p. 7; Hobley, 1910, p. 238

[88] Maxwell Report, Appendix, pp. 16, 46; Hobley, 1938, p. 179; Leakey, 1, 1934; Beecher, 1944, p. 4.

[89] Routledge, 1910, p. 20.

[90] K. R. Dundas, 1, 1908, p. 138; Lindblom, 1920, p. 114; Lambert, 2, 1947, pp. 31 ff.; K.L.C. Evidence, 1932, II, p. 1,292.

[91] Tate, 1910, p. 237; Maxwell Report, 1929, Appendix, p. 46; Routledge, 1910, p. 20.

[92] C. Dundas, 1915, pp. 266–7; Hobley, 1938, p. 119.

[93] Kenyatta, 1938, p. 227; Routledge, 1910, p. 196; Cagnolo, 1933, p. 100; C. Dundas, 1915, pp. 237, 239; Boyes, 1911, p. 91.

[94] Kenyatta, 1938, pp. 2, 138, 151; Maxwell Report, 1929, Appendix, pp. 7, 9, 36; Hobley, 1910, p. 136; 1938, p. 260.

which are wider than the *mbari* and narrower than the sub-clan, which must be of fairly large size, although there is no specific evidence on this point.

Beecher states that each sub-clan has "certain characteristic customs of its own", but he does not say what these are. There is some evidence that clans have certain distinctive features as well as different totemic beliefs. According to Cagnolo, each has a "characteristic exclamation", and Routledge says that they have different traditions, especially as regards food taboos (he may be referring to totemic taboos). Hobley states that each clan has a mark which is put on bee-hives and the trees in which they are set, and there are various occupations which are peculiar or forbidden to certain clans: the Agaciku may not work iron nor act as circumcision operators; the Aceera and Anjiru are noted for their powers of sorcery and the evil eye; and the Aithaga have strong magical powers. The Aithaga clan consists of two sections, one of which contains rain-makers and the other "wizards". These powers are held only by males; women marry into their own clan, although a man will sometimes marry outside. Clans have no distinctive dress or ornaments.[95]

The Mbari

A *mbari* is a descent group which may be of considerable depth (7 or 8 known generations), mostly named after its founder or one of its founders, and owning jointly a piece of land, its *githaka*.

The Kikuyu system of land tenure is often referred to as "the *githaka* system". The Maxwell Report states: "We have defined *githaka* as the Kikuyu unit of land tenure. A *githaka* today may consist of entirely bush or forest land, entirely cultivated land or some of each. Its original sense was bushland but it has come to have the above technical sense."[96]

The Kiambu Kikuyu acquired the land from the Dorobo mostly through purchase. In the north, first clearing came to be regarded as a proof of ownership.

Kenyatta states that the two types of claim to a piece of land, by clearing or by purchase from the Dorobo, are the same in principle; the Dorobo's rights based on first clearing were purchased.[97]

A *githaka* need not be cultivated in its entirety, but may include fallow, grazing and virgin soil. Neither need the *githaka* be in one continuous piece, but may consist of several plots of land interspersed among the plots of other *mbari*. These sub-plots are also called *ithaka*.[98]

Rights over a piece of land, claimed by first clearing or purchase, can be held first by one individual, or by a group of individuals. Men belonging to one *mbari* of origin might band together and buy from the Dorobo and thus found a new *mbari*, but men from different *mbari* and even different *mihiriga* could do the same and thus found a new *mbari*. For *mbari* purposes (legal and ceremonial) they would adopt the *muhiriga* of one of the founders and the *mbari* would acquire one name: the name of an ancestor of one of the founders or in some cases the name of an important powerful man, not related in any direct sense. When land was thus bought jointly there are within the *mbari* a number of *nyumba* or houses, called after the actual founders of the *nyumba* who participated in the buying.

If land had been bought by one individual it became known as the *githaka* of the *mbari* of X after it had been inherited for the first time. The *mbari* of one founder did not come into existence until after his death.[99]

Each *mbari* selected from among its most able members a *muramati*, a leader of the mbari in matters of land. His chief duty was to control the allocation and use of

[95] Beecher, 1944, p. 4; Cagnolo, 1933, pp. 21, 135; Routledge, 1910, pp. 20–2; Hobley, 1938, pp. 177–83, 253–4. See below, p. 66, for a description of the magical powers of the Aithaga clan.

[96] Maxwell Report, 1929, p. 69; see also Barlow, 1932, p. 57; Liversage, 1945, p. 4. The plural of *githaka* is *ithaka*.

[97] C. Dundas, 1915, p. 297; 1921, p. 272; Maxwell Report, 1929, p. 6; Hobley, 1938, p. 146; Kenyatta, 1938, p. 27.

[98] Barlow, 1932, p. 60; Maxwell Report, 1929, Appendix, p. 39.

[99] Kenyatta, 1938, pp. 29–32; Maxwell Report, 1929, p. 16.

the land. He need not be the most senior member of the group concerned although this was often the case. The *muramati*, as far as can be ascertained, had no more cultivation or building rights than his brothers. He had the power to adjust the allotment of holdings with the *mbari* and to admit or refuse tenants.[100]

The *muramati* allocated land to the *mbari*-segments, the component domestic families; the principles on which the allotment was made were those of need and of matri-segmentation; that is to say, the founders of the component families of the *mbari* inherited their plots of land from their mothers' "houses", and any resulting maldistribution was corrected by the *muramati* when a family is short of land. Land allotted included arable, grazing, forest and other "reserved" land.

All male, circumcised and married members of the *mbari* formed a council: the *kiama kia ndundu* or *kiama kia mbari*, which under the leadership of the *muramati* regulated *mbari* affairs.

There is some evidence that within the *mbari* the proximity of the *mbari* segment to the founding segment of the *mbari* was important in making certain decisions.

Under the Kikuyu system, the boundaries of a *githaka* were fixed according to the original claims by the *mbari* founder. In many cases they acquired more land than they needed for their immediate wants, but still overcrowding or conflict might create the need for acquiring extra land in ownership or rights of use in land of other *mbari*. A segment of the *mbari* might split off and move to new unclaimed land elsewhere. It could retain the name of the *mbari* of origin or found a new *mbari*. In both cases it would remain linked with its *mbari* of origin in certain situations such as exogamy, feuds and warfare and assistance in murder fines. This applied for a number of generations, but it is as yet unknown to what extent co-operation existed and whether there were significant differences in co-operation between *mbari* continuing to have the same names and between *mbari* of which segments had chosen different names. Segments could also buy land from other already existing *mbari* provided those *mbari* did not have a prohibition to sell their land through a testamentary statement (*kirumi*) made by either a founder or by a senior elder at a later stage of *mbari* development. Sales were outright in Kiambu, but redeemable in Fort Hall.

An individual or a *mbari* segment might also acquire rights of use in land of other existing *mbari*; they would then become tenants, *ahoi* (sing. *muhoi*) or *athami* (sing. *muthami*) or in a small number of cases *aguri* (sing. *muguri*). For the differences between these types of tenancy we refer to the section on land tenure.

Many *mbari*, especially the larger ones in Kiambu, had given tenancy rights to non-*mbari* members: a territorial unit, whether *ituura* or *rugongo*, might thus comprise one *mbari*, or several *mbari*, closely related or not, with or without tenants. Within a *mbari* are the *nyumba*, the "houses" of each of the founders of the *mbari* or of the sons or brothers of one founder. The same word *nyumba* is also used for each elementary or polygynous domestic family living in the homestead, the *mucii*, as well as for a woman's hut.[101]

The unity of the *nyumba* which are segments of one *mbari* appeared in their submission to the authority of a common *muramati* in matters of land (in large *mbari* each constituent *nyumba* might have its own *muramati*, but all would recognize the supreme authority of the joint *muramati*), in common sacrifices and above all in its joint interest in the common patrimonial land. It is implicit in all references to the *mbari* that it cannot be regarded as a unit apart from its land.

Mbari vary widely in size. There seems to be no recent information but the sizes of 109 *mbari* can be reckoned from the précis of claims of several hundred *mbari* for land alienated from them, which are given on pp. 268-375 of the Kenya Land Commission Evidence, Vol. I.[102] Frequencies are:

[100] Maxwell Report, 1929. Appendix, p. 37; also Report, p. 9; Kenyatta, 1938, p. 33.

[101] Kenyatta, 1938, pp. 1, 53, 77; Routledge, 1910, p. 117.

[102] Figures are taken from the individual evidence of several hundred heads of families.

Total membership	1–100	101–200	201–300	301–400	401–500	501–600	601–700	701–800	801–900	901–1000	1001–2000	2001 plus
No. of *mbari*	12	19	13	12	11	9	4	3	8	8	5	5

The smallest *mbari* consisted of 32 persons, and the largest of 5,000. The mode lies between 101 and 200 persons.[103] In the case of 33 *mbari* where detailed membership is given, the mean number of men in each *mbari* is 72·5, of women 110·3, and of children 246. Clearly many of the *mbari* shown in this evidence were too large to be joint families. Kenyatta and others state that generally a *mbari* consists of the descendants of a common grandfather and great-grandfather.[104] The Maxwell Report states that today in Kiambu there are still certain *mbari* which hold their land in common and have never sub-divided it.[105] Land consolidation executed since 1954 has had as a consequence that *mbari* land has been divided into individual holdings: this does not mean however that all important aspects of the *mbari* have ceased to exist.

Mbari expansion could be achieved through natural growth as well as through systems in which outsiders were recruited as members. A man might give his daughter in marriage to a person without asking for bridewealth (*ruracio*); he might also "adopt" unaligned young boys who would later marry members of his *mbari*, again without *ruracio*, or give under the same conditions his daughter to a *ndungata* (a poor man who acted as resident labourer, not belonging to the *mbari*). In all these cases offspring born belonged to the *mbari* of the owner, not to the physical father. There is evidence that in the sales of land from the Dorobo to the Kikuyu this type of adoption played a role, but this "adoption" should not be confused with the mutual ceremony of adoption between Dorobo and Kikuyu which had to take place before land transactions between them could be effected.

During the period of rapid Kikuyu expansion in the latter half of the 18th and the 19th century *mbari* expansion was important.

Mbari would seem to be structurally similar, differences in size being due to different stages in their cycle of development and fission.

Settlement Pattern and Homestead[106]

The homestead (*mucii*) was the home of the domestic family. Each homestead had its enclosure, and formerly each was surrounded by a high green hedge or stockade, entered by a low doorway. In the compound made by the stockade the cattle were kept at night. Large households might have two compounds, an inner and an outer. Within the homestead enclosure each wife had her own hut; where there were several wives the husband had a hut of his own.

In Kikuyu the "bachelor hut" (*thingira*) was characteristic. Routledge states that it might stand apart from the homestead, and was the sleeping-place of the boys from several homesteads, as well as the "guest-house". It may be assumed that there was

[103] This is confirmed by figures derived from other evidence: the Maxwell Report states that *ithaka* vary from 50 to 6,000 acres, the "average" being between 200 and 300 acres (Maxwell Report, p. 9); the K.L.C. Evidence states that the average acreage per head in 1931 was 2·17 acres in Fort Hall and 1·60 in Nyeri (K.L.C. Evidence, 1932, I, p. 974). The Maxwell Report figures apply to South Nyeri. From these figures it may be computed that when applied to Fort Hall the average *githaka* contains approximately between 91 and 136 persons, and applied to Nyeri, between 125 and 188 persons. These will include residential tenants, but they may be taken as a rough approximation.

[104] Kenyatta 1938, p. 235; Barlow, 1938, p. 60; Tate, 2, 1940, p. 256.

[105] Maxwell Report 1929, Appendix, p. 52.

[106] See Routledge, 1910, pp. 48, 49, 117–18; Cagnolo, 1933, pp. 33, 54–6, 115; Kenyatta, 1938, pp. 79, 82–4, 117; Boyes, 1911, p. 303; Champion, 1912, pp. 72–4; Orde-Browne, 1925, pp. 111–16; Tate, 1, 1904, p. 131; 2, 1904, p. 256; von Höhnel, 1894, p. 318; Jackson, 1930, p. 172; MacDonald, 1897, p. 110; Crawshay, 1902, p. 34; Laughton, 1944, p. 9.

one *thingira* for each joint family, perhaps attached to the homestead of its head. The *thingira* was used for the pre-marital sexual relations of warriors and girls. A similar institution existed in Meru, Chuka, Mwimbi and Tharaka: in the three forme tribes the hut was known as *ngaaro*. The *ngaaro* was larger than the Kikuyu *thingir* and was of special construction and decoration. In Embu uncircumcised boys slep in their mothers' huts until they became warriors, when they lived in small huts c their own. The living arrangements differed slightly among all the Northern tribes.[107]

Homesteads were scattered across the country, not grouped in large clusters The *ituura* or "village" of the joint family consisted of several groups of home steads. The word "village" is misleading, since it has the connotation of a territoriall compact group, but its use has become customary. Homesteads were usually built o hillsides or in wooded areas and were formerly often protected by war-pits. Th actual site was carefully chosen: it might not be connected with any ancestral curs or taboo, nor be on or near a grave or battle-place where spirits might live.[108]

Each wife possessed her own granary, placed near her hut in Kikuyu, but amon the Northern tribes usually outside the enclosure, since unthreshed grain might no be brought into the village. Each homestead had a trough of saline earth for th goats.

In the centre of the hut was the fireplace of three stones. The wall space was par titioned off by sticks into small compartments, containing the beds made of plank or interwoven sticks, and store-places. The outer compartment among the Kikuyu wa used for the goats at night, but among the Northern tribes the huts were smaller an the goats were usually given a separate hut.[109]

There is little information about differences between the patterns of settlement i Kikuyu and the Northern tribes. Lambert, referring principally to the Meru, state that they lived in very small "villages" each containing the homesteads of a join family of up to three generations. Married sons usually set up their own homestead on their father's land if there was room for them. Each married woman had her ow separate hut and garden, but mutual help in agricultural work was general.[110]

"Villages" in the sense of territorially compact groups were introduced by th colonial government during the Mau Mau Emergency. They were intended to giv greater security to the population as well as greater control over it. Land consolidatio is said to have been facilitated by removing the scattered clusters of people into mor concentrated areas. In the latter part of the Emergency a start was made to provid the villagers with certain amenities such as wells for water, village halls for meetings nursery schools, etc. As a rule the village was populated by people who had been livin in the immediate neighbourhood together with people who could claim a relationshi with them and who were "repatriated" from such areas as Nairobi, the Europea farming area and Tanganyika, during the Emergency. Sometimes villages wer inhabited by one large kin group, sometimes by several smaller ones as nuclei aroun which affinal relations and people related neither through land nor through marriag could be grouped.

At the end of the Emergency farmers who owned a certain "economic" acreag were allowed to resettle on their then consolidated holdings; later everyone wa permitted to choose his own dwelling area. At the moment a number of farmers hav returned to their holdings, mostly with their nuclear family only. Sometimes they have given permission to build on their farms to dependent collateral or affina relatives, to labourers or to others to whom they are bound by obligations of friend

[107] Routledge, 1910, pp. 117–18; Cagnolo, 1933, pp. 55, 56, 115; Kenyatta, 1938, p. 177 Boyes, 1911, p. 303; Champion, 1912, pp. 72, 74; Orde-Browne, 1925, pp. 113–16; Tate, 2, 1904 p. 256.

[108] Cagnolo, 1933, pp. 25, 33; Tate, 1, 1904, p. 131; von Höhnel, 1894, I, p. 318; Jackson 1930, p. 172; MacDonald, 1897, p. 110, Kenyatta, 1938, p. 79.

[109] Routledge, 1910, pp. 48, 59, 118; Cagnolo, 1933, pp. 33, 54; von Höhnel, 1894, I, p. 318; Crawshay, 1902, p. 34; Champion, 1912, pp. 72–3; Laughton, 1944, pp. 9; Kenyatta, 1938 pp. 82–4; Orde-Browne, 1925, pp. 111–12.

[110] Lambert, 1947, p. 3.

hip. Many people have stayed in the villages for economic reasons or from personal reference. The situation is still too fluid and insufficient data are available to speak f any definite patterning of the settlement.[111]

Kikuyu Territorial System

The smallest grouping was the elementary or polygynous domestic family living n the homestead (*mucii*). A group of *micii* might form an *ituura*, which has often een translated by "village".[112] An *ituura* might be inhabited by one *mbari*, part of a *nbari*, with or without *ahoi*, or by several *mbari*. Dundas states that the *ituura* was ometimes referred to as *thome*[113], and that often the members of a *thome*; or a najority of them, were of one "clan"; thus the *thome* was referred to as the place of uch and such a "clan". Leakey and Lambert state that a group of *ituura* formed a *nwaki*, a unit in which people would assist each other with hot embers to re-light a re (*mwaki*) which had gone out.[114] Again, the *mwaki* was not necessarily the home of ne *mbari*, but could comprise parts of several *mbari*, with or without *ahoi*. *Miaki* in heir turn again would be part of a *rugongo*, a ridge.

The relationship between the characteristic ridge formation of the country and he territorial organization can be inferred with fair certainty. A *mbari*, it seems, was sually considered as dwelling on a ridge, a *rugongo*. The interpretation of the early vidence is made more difficult by a too close identification of the *mbari* and the *ugongo*.[115]

Hobley has a statement which might be taken to mean that the ridge was the ome of the *mbari*: "Up to comparatively recent times, each clan is said to have nhabited its own location. In recent years, however, the clans have become much roken up and intermingled and the result has been to substitute the ridge for the lan. . . . Each ridge keeps more or less to itself with its own chiefs, its own plantaions and its own grazing grounds."[116]

Hobley, however, implies elsewhere that a ridge was a larger unit than the *nbari*: it would seem to be a district or territorial group composed of several *mbari*. The Maxwell Report also gives weight to this interpretation, since it states that an *nbari* occupied "part of a ridge".[117]

Dundas states that the original Kikuyu settlers opened up the land ridge by ridge nd became the founders of *mbari*. Bugeau writes that a group of homesteads (*mucii*) ormed what is called a *rugongo* or ridge. This is supported by Hobley and Phillips.

The *rugongo* might be the home of one *mbari*, with or without tenants, or of everal *mbari*, with or without tenants. It was, however, a defined unit for political, ocial and ritual purposes which transcendes the interest of the *mbari*. Kenyatta, lescribing sacrifices to God, writes: "Thus people living between one river and nother are considered to constitute a sacrificial unit. They have one sacred tree or grove under which they offer sacrifices in common."[118] These sacred groves or trees are listinct from the sacred trees of *mbari*. Evidence from early travellers clearly indiates the separate nature of the *ng'ongo*. Von Höhnel wrote that at every one of the treams he crossed he had to pay tribute, each small valley having its own 'Samaki",[119] and he adds that the streams were clearly the boundaries of units and hat the "chief" of each valley was the "chief of a village".[120]

[111] Pedraza, 1956; Penwill, 1960; Leakey, 1956; Channon, 1955, 1957; Hughes, 1955, Kolbe nd Fouche, 1959.

[112] Hobley, 1938, p. 94; Kenyatta, 1938, p. 194; C. Dundas, 1915, pp. 239, 248, uses 'village" for the home of the elementary family.

[113] The word is derived from the open space in front of a village, see C. Dundas, 1915, p. 239.

[114] Leakey, 1952, p. 36, 37; Lambert, 1956, p. 108, 109.

[115] Leakey, 1952, p. 34.

[116] Hobley, 2, 1910, p. 138.

[117] Hobley, 1938, p. 47; Maxwell Report, 1929, Appendix, p. 19.

[118] Kenyatta, 1938, pp. 245–6.

[119] Von Höhnel, 1894, I, p. 309. "Samaki" is clearly the word *muthamaki*, the term used or an elder or council of elders, representative or spokesman.

[120] Von Höhnel, pp. 316, 344. See also Boyes, 1911, p. 91.

Most of the authorities refer to wider territorial groupings, usually calle "districts".[121] Such a district might be called *bururi*, although the word usually refer to the three large territorial divisions of Kikuyuland (Kiambu, Fort Hall and Nyeri or to the whole of Kikuyu territory.

Dundas states that geographical and historical circumstances have "tended t cut up the tribe into a multitude of sections, each of which has some slight distinguish ing peculiarity of custom. The extension of these groups is in general discernible b the *rika* or circumcision ages."[122] He adds that there were common foci of interes which form ties extending beyond the *mbari*, the most important being the commo places of sacrifice.[123] It seems from Routledge that a district consisted of from 5 t 30 *mbari*, the chief bond being "the advice of one medicine man".[124]

The district was also the unit on which the age-sets and part of the judicia system of the Kikuyu were based. It is not easy to discover the span of these districts that is, the area over which representatives of local councils of elders had authority and over which according to Dundas, the *mbari* sacrificed to God simultaneously.

Dundas writes, when discussing the districts as units for circumcision-sets: " am speaking . . . of communities, as distinct from sections of the tribe between whic there was formerly often great hostility, as . . . between Tetu and Ndia Kikuyu."[1 These "sections" were Divisions or Districts in the colonial government system, an were very considerable groupings, each consisting of many thousand people.[126] It ca be taken, therefore, that the indigenous districts were smaller than the colonia government Divisions or Sections, but there is no way of telling how large the actually were.

Groupings of wider extent, the *bururi* proper of Kiambu, Fort Hall and Nyer existed, but it is impossible to discover from the available material to what exten they acted as groups.

There is no evidence that they ever united in war, even against neighbourin tribes. Dundas suggests that the *ituika* ceremony probably provided an occasion fo the most extensive combination known among the Kikuyu[127]; in the district nov known as Nyeri there seem to have been only three areas having separate *matuika* these are the Sections (colonial government Divisions) of Tetu, Ndia and Mathira These Divisions are clearly recognized by the Kikuyu as part of the Kikuyu proper as opposed to Embu and Meru, the inhabitants of which are not claimed as Kikuy and cannot be admitted as tenants on Kikuyu land, according to the Maxwe Report.[128]

In the last instance *bururi* can refer to the whole of Kikuyu country. In using i in this way expression is given to the sense of all Kikuyu as "children of Gikuy and Muumbi", who from the beginning have set forth and acquired the Kikuy territory. Kenyatta refers to *bururi wa Gikuyu* which he translates as "territory of th Kikuyu" and which he says means the actual Kikuyu land as a symbol of triba unity.[129] The fact that there were certain institutions which stretch across all Kikuy proper (but not into Embu) also points to this realization of unity. These institution were the *mihiriga*, the age- or status-grades, the age-sets and the generation-se system and a system of what have been called "guilds".[130]

There are a few references to parts of Kikuyu country which are vaguely defined

[121] The term "district" is confusing owing to pre-independence division of Kikuyu int five administrative Districts, which are quite different units. We shall keep the term, but us the lower case only, and keep the capital letter for the previous administrative Districts.

[122] C. Dundas, 1915, p. 240.
[123] C. Dundas, 1915, p. 240.
[124] Routledge, 1910, p. 196.
[125] Dundas, 1915, p. 240; see also p. 247.
[126] Phillips, 1945, p. 37, implies that the districts and the modern Divisions are the same he appears to be incorrect on this point.
[127] C. Dundas, 1915, p. 247; see below, pp. 37–8.
[128] Maxwell Report, 1929, p. 6.
[129] Kenyatta, 1938, p. 22.
[130] These systems are described below.

These include *Metumi*, Kikuyu north of the Chania; *Karura*, south of the Chania; and *Kaki*, *Ruguru* (West Kikuyu), and *Itherero* (East Kikuyu).[131]

Although there seem to be no functional groupings wider than the district, there are certain focal points for inter-district combination. These include markets, which Routledge calls "rallying points for several districts"[132]; others may be public grazing grounds, salt-licks, etc.[133] Rivers which form inter-district boundaries and which serve the livestock of both banks might also be classified under this heading.

It seems clear that within the *ituura* political office was held by the council of elders, *athuuri*, to which all men who held the grade of *muthuuri*[134] belonged, irrespective of whether they were members of the local *mbari* or *ahoi*. Several important questions are however still under research, such as the extent to which position of seniority within the *mbari* or the fact that a *muthuuri* might be a *muhoi* would influence the weight given to his voice. It seems likely that this differed with the matter which was under discussion. Another important problem is the influence of the generation-set system within the council.[135] It seems likely that important laws could only be made by elders who belonged to the "ruling" generation-set, although attention would have to be paid to elders of other sets.[136]

Elders' councils would select a leader or spokesman from among themselves and this office could certainly be held by a man who was not a member of the local *mbari*. Whether he had to be a member of the ruling generation-set is still uncertain.

This leader was, however, not a "chief" in any sense. Councils would seek to select a man who was known for his wisdom, a *muthamaki*, who could advise through his experience and command respect. These *athamaki* might in certain cases obtain renown far beyond their local councils and be sought after as arbiters in disputes within the *rugongo* and even wider. If a *muthamaki* was moreover a senior member of the *mbari* with unused land at his disposal, then tenants would seek to come and live with him. He might thus be a very influential person, and also a very wealthy one. As such it was likely that his position within the council was of great importance. But as leader of the council he had to communicate and in certain cases to execute the will of the council, in whose decisions he had only one voice, although an important one.

Many of the writers on the Kikuyu mention chiefs, and the same names of chiefs occur in many different sources: at the beginning of the century there seem to have been some half dozen leaders who apparently held sway over very considerable areas. The names of Karuri, Wang'ombe, Nduini and Gakeri in the north, Kinyanjui in Kiambu and Karuri in west Kikuyu often occur.[137] It seems likely that these "chiefs" were important men in the indigenous system and were chosen by the early administrators as chiefs over large districts, their duties being to keep general law and order, provide carriers and so on. But Dundas writes: "I feel convinced that these tribes had no heads or leaders who could be dignified with the name of chief. . . . Those who suppose that chiefs formerly did exist have been unable to discover any powers, distinctions, privileges, or marks distinguishing the chiefs from their subjects. . . . I will not say that there were no individuals more prominent than others; some were respected for their wisdom or wealth, medicine men gained a certain importance in proportion to their real or supposed abilities, and so also the *muthigani* (war leader) could not fail to become a prominent figure, though, perhaps, equal respect was accorded to the experienced leader of hunting parties and trading caravans. Even particular charms could command obedience. . . . Whether at any time there were heads of clans exercising authority over the clansmen it is impossible

[131] Lambert, 1950, p. 4; Hobley, 1938, p. 105; K. R. Dundas, 1909, p. 38.

[132] Routledge, 1910, p. 197.

[133] See below, p. 52.

[134] See the part on age or status grades.

[135] See the part on generation-sets.

[136] Lambert, 1956, p. 131.

[137] Middleton, 1965.

to say." Leakey states categorically that there were no indigenous chiefs. The present-day chiefs are government-appointed.[138]

It is, however, clear that in pre-European times as well as later elders belonging to important, long-established and powerful *mbari* could command influence far beyond their *mbari* or their territorial unit. These *athamaki* were prominent people of wide renown.

Dundas refers to the importance of each elder in his own village, and points out that "when they met in council they represented for the community what each one counted for in his village. Thus custom, law and religion were all in the hands of the elders. . . . When the assembly (of elders) met for judicial purposes it was called a *kiama*. But in practice there was no distinction between those who legislated, judged or acted as priests for the people—there were only various duties vested in the fathers of the people, and nothing could supersede their standing".[139]

It would seem that the elders' grades stretched across a district; districts were the units concerned in the ceremonies to do with entrance to the various grades. An elder was recognized as an elder in his own district; although his rank might be recognized outside it, it can be assumed that his political powers could not be exercised beyond his district's borders. This is not to say, however, that the councils which met to arbitrate at cases invariably consisted of all the elders of a given district. Hobley states that before the British administration "there appear to have been no fixed councils or meeting places, which is easily explained by the fact that there were no definite locations. If two men had a case, they each called a few elders who met to judge the case". Kenyatta writes that there were several recognized meeting places.[140] These would all be within the area under the jurisdiction of one group of elders.

When matters of wider importance than *ituura* interest were involved, representatives of each *ituura* council would meet to form councils of wider units. Leakey describes a highly decentralized system of government in which the *matuura*, *miaki* and the *ng'ongo* had their own elected or appointed councils of elders, while matters affecting several *ng'ongo* would be dealt with by special *ad hoc* councils formed by representatives of the *ng'ongo* involved.[141] Phillips and Kenyatta mention the *kiama* of *mucii*, *ituura* and *rugongo*.[142] More data are however still needed to analyse the nature of the recruitment into these councils, their functions and authority in the different spheres of the social and political system, and the influence of the generation-set system on their recruitment and authority.

Kikuyu Age-grades or Status-grades

The Kikuyu have a system of age-grades or status-grades which cover the whole of each individual's life. People pass through these different status groups, irrespective of whether they are part of a local *mbari* or its tenants. Each grade has its own rights and duties within the community, and a descriptive term indicates the status of the individual.[143] This system has now virtually died out. However, we use the "ethnographic present" tense throughout.

Men:

Gakenge	Baby boy
Kahi	Small boy
Kihi	Uncircumcised boy
Muumo	Circumcised youth
Mwanake	Warrior, adult man
Muthuuri	Elder or elderly man

[138] C. Dundas, 1915, p. 238; Leakey, 2, 1934; Hobley, 1938, pp. 307, 314–15; Stigand, 1913, p. 234; Hall, 1938, *passim*; Hailey, 1950, Part I, *passim*.

[139] C. Dundas, 1915, pp. 248–9.

[140] Phillips, 1945, pp. 37–8; Champion, 1912, p. 87; Hobley, 1938, p. 215; Cagnolo, 1933, p. 147; Kenyatta, 183, p. 217; Tate, 1910, pp. 245–6; 1911, p. 294.

[141] Leakey, 1952, p. 36.

[142] Phillips, 1945, pp. 38, 64; Kenyatta, 1938, pp. 35, 194.

[143] Routledge, 1910, pp. 25, 141; Hobley, 1938, p. 209; Tate, 1911, pp. 290–1; K. R. Dundas, 2, 1908, pp. 180–1; Lambert, 1956, pp. 1–7.

Women:

Kaana Baby girl
Karigu Small girl
Kirigu Uninitiated girl
Kairitu Initiated girl
Muhiki Betrothed or married woman without child
Wabai Mother of young children
Mutumia Mother of one or more initiated children
Kiheti Toothless old woman

The uninitiated boy, *kihi*, has no rights of possession and is not regarded as a full member of the community; he may not have his own homestead nor take part in fighting. He may not wear the long hair of the circumcised youth; he may not have sexual relations with initiated girls nor have a circumcised youth as a friend. A circumcised youth, *mwanake*, may inherit property, and spends his time dancing and thinking of marriage. He is a full adult member of the tribe.[144] Circumcised boys are visited by girls in the *thingira* or bachelor hut; the girls bring food which is "shared among the age-group in the *thingira*, who eat their food collectively."[145] Sexual relationship between the warriors and girls is known as *nguiko*: this is a form of sexual intimacy without intercourse, the latter being punishable. Brother and sister must not be together in the *thingira* except on occasions when there is no *nguiko*, nor may they dance together. This prohibition extends to "cousins".[146]

After initiation the *mwanake* joins in the council of *anake*: the *kiama kia ita* (the council of war). In some Kikuyu areas this council knew two divisions: the *kiama kia aanake a muumo* or junior council of *aanake* and only after having paid the several fees connected with the life of *aanake* would they belong to the council of *aanake* proper.[147]

During the first stage of being *aanake* the young men would be provided by their fathers with arms, and the payment of fees was accompanied by the attainment of progressively more important rights.[148]

The *kiama kia ita* could not itself take the decision to engage in raiding or actual warfare, it had to obtain permission of the *athuuri*, and favourable advice from the *mundu mugo wa ita*, a ritual specialist for warfare. The internal organization of the *kiama kia ita* will be discussed in the section on age-sets.

Warriors will after marriage, and mostly shortly after the birth of a child, seek to enter into the status of *athuuri* (sing. *muthuuri*) or elders. As such they become members of the council of elders, the *kiama kia athuuri*, discussed under the territorial organization. At a first payment of one goat a *mwanake* becomes a *muthuuri wa mburi imwe*, an elder of the first goat, or *kamatimu*. He is not yet a full fledged elder but he becomes a member of the junior part of the *kiama kia athuuri*, the *kiama kia kamatimu*.[149] The members of this council are regarded as "learners" to the *kiama kia athuuri* or *kiama kia athamaki*[150] for which they act as messengers and general helpers. On the payment of a second goat, mostly when the first child of a *kamatimu* is about to be circumcised, he becomes a full member of the *kiama*, a *muthuuri wa mburi igiri*: he is given a staff, the *muthigi*, and is allowed to carry *matathi* leaves.[151] There is

[144] Kenyatta, 1938, pp. 107–8; Cagnolo, 1933, pp. 97–9; Bugeau, 1911, p. 617.

[145] Kenyatta, 1938, p. 157; a problem which arises is that of the relationship between the age-set who use the *thingira* and the *mbari* at whose chief homestead it is apparently built.

[146] Kenyatta, 1938, pp. 158–61; Leakey, 1931, pp. 277–8; C. Dundas, 1915, p. 273; 1921, p. 247; Orde-Browne, 1925, p. 70.

[147] Kenyatta, 1938, pp. 198 ff. Lambert, 1956, pp. 78.

[148] Lambert, 1956, pp. 85–87.

[149] *Kamatimu* either means "those who sit away" (from the main council), Hobley, 1938; p. 211, or the word comes from *matimu* (spear) "which denotes the warriors who have joined the *kiama* while still functioning as warriors, and who are carrying spears because they have not been given the staff of office." (Kenyatta, 1938, pp. 200–1).

[150] *Muthamaki* is variously translated as "senior elder", "wise man" or "leader".

[151] Hobley, 1938, p. 210; Kenyatta, 1930, pp. 108, 201; C. Dundas, 1915, p. 243; Lambert, 1956, p. 83.

considerable confusion in the literature about payment of goats and the sub-division of eldership status.[152] Within each sub-group, such as *kamatimu* or *athuuri wa mburi igiri* goats have to be paid at various intervals and situations; in some districts they are the condition upon which an elder reaches the next status group, in others they are payments made within one status-group. This is probably also the explanation of the fact that some writers recognize three, four or five different stages of eldership. Also, considerable difference exists in the districts about the stages of eldership themselves.[153]

Part of the confusion is also due to the fact that several different terms are used for the office of an elder of any grade within either of the councils, depending on whether reference is made to his actual status, the insignia of office, or to the number of goats he has paid to enter the grade.

A small number of elders will reach, mostly in later life, the most senior stage of eldership in which they became members of the *kiama kia maturanguru*. *Maturanguru* are sacred leaves which are carried as badge of office. These elders are entrusted with the ceremonial and religious affairs of the community, they lead the *igongona* (sacrifice) for the community, can remove *thahu* (ritual uncleanliness) and curse evildoers; other functions are to decide the dates of circumcisions and the holding of the *ituika* ceremony.[154] They form the *ndundu* or "inner council" at the arbitration of legal cases.

Kiama would exist on the *ituura, mwaki* and *rugongo* level. Leakey states that the elders of the *ituura* form a council of nine elders, which appoint another council of nine elders to represent the *ituura* within one *mwaki*; the elders of the *miaki* within one *rugongo* in their turn elect the *kiama kinene* (big council) of nine elders which controls the affairs of the *rugongo*.[155]

Lambert does not mention this hierarchical system but states that the elders of the *kiama kinene* are elders who have paid three goats (*athuuri wa mburi ithatu*). His *kiama kinene* deal with the more serious legal cases and with the affairs of the *rugongo*.[156] Whether Leakey's data refer to an earlier stage of Kikuyu development and Lambert to a later stage or whether there was considerable local difference in the working of the *kiama* is uncertain.

Kenyatta and Hobley give descriptions of the ceremony of admittance from one grade to another.[157]

There is a parallel system for women, referred to constantly in the literature, but there is little explicit information. Hobley states that there is a *kiama* of old women in every district, who seem to have disciplinary powers over women, and who are feared on account of their powers of witchcraft.[158] Lambert mentions the *kiama kia aka*,[159] a council of women, but more information on the subject is still needed.

According to the various authorities, the qualifications for entry in the various grades are age, wealth and personal wisdom.[160] Routledge states that social seniority measured by genealogical status and maturity of the applicant's children, not biological age, is the criterion.[161] This would appear to be generally true, especially as regards the junior grades and those of the elders of *matathi*. The crucial point is the criterion for entry into the grade of elders of *maturanguru*. Kenyatta states that this grade is reached when the applicant's wife is past child-bearing. Hobley writes that generally the sacrificial elders are men advanced in years, but that they may often

[152] Kenyatta, 1938, p. 108; Routledge, 1910, pp. 197–9; C. Dundas, 1915, pp. 243–4; Hobley, 1938, p. 211; Phillips, 1945, p. 37; Lambert, 1956, pp. 80–97.

[153] Lambert, 1956; p. 88.

[154] Hobley, 1938, pp. 211–12; C. Dundas, 1915, p. 243; Kenyatta, 1938, pp. 108, 204–205. According to Lambert, 1956, p. 89.

[155] Leakey, 1952, 35, 36.

[156] Lambert, 1956, p. 83, 84.

[157] Kenyatta, 1938, pp. 201–3; Hobley, 1938, pp 209–14.

[158] Hobley, 1938, p. 274; Kenyatta, 1938, pp. 111–12.

[159] Lambert, 1956, 95–100.

[160] See C. Dundas, 1915, p. 244; Cagnolo, 1933, p. 25; Routledge, p. 206.

[161] Routledge, 1910, p. 197.

include young men: he explains this by saying that the sacrificial elders will co-opt any likely young men who are renowned for their wisdom.[162] He adds: "The family of a *muthamaki*[163] should always be represented in this grade, and therefore if one dies and leaves no near relation other than a young man, they will elect his son or brother in his place even if he is quite a youth."[164] Tate states that "if a chief is very old his son may become . . . an elder with authority to determine cases in the native councils, as soon as he has been circumcised and is sufficiently experienced and capable." Stigand writes that if a member of the *kiama* dies, he is replaced by another.[165]

Although all *kiama kia athuuri* contain local elders regardless of whether they belong to the local *mbari* or are *ahoi*, there are some indications that in the senior grade of elders *mbari*-membership plays an important role as well as membership of the generation-set in power.[166] To a large extent the status of the individual within the *mbari* regulates his status within other groups. A man important in his *mbari* may have to move more quickly through the status grades than a tenant and special fees are demanded by the status grade for this process.

The Kikuyu Age-sets and the Generation-set System

The Kikuyu have two other important institutions, which cut across *mbari* and *muhiriga* affiliations. They are the age-sets and the generation-sets, both called *marika* (sing. *rika*). The component parts of the age-sets, the circumcision years, are also called *marika*. It is probable that the *marika* are the most effective forms of tribal cohesion.

The age-sets are named, corporate groups, with leaders and fixed membership recruited between defined times and for a specific period and purpose. They do not form a system, as they release their members into the different age-grades or status-grades, mentioned above, individually independent of the age-set as a whole. After a certain time the age-set as a whole does not act as a corporate group, although small segments of it (one circumcision year, or boys circumcised at the same homestead during one circumcision) may continue to act as a corporate group for defined purposes.

An age-set is composed of a number of sub-sets, or circumcision years. The Kikuyu traditionally practise male and female circumcision, the latter taking place every year as it is important that a girl was circumcised before reaching puberty. Circumcision for boys takes place at a number of consecutive years followed by a "closed period" (*muhingo*) of a number of years, probably 4½ years or nine seasons, but this varies. Each circumcision year is given a name, the names chosen referring to some outstanding event of the year. Hobley states that the system of named sets applies only to males and does not refer to girls' age-sets. The names for any one year may vary over different parts of the country, as can be seen from the available lists. How far differently named *rika* are regarded as being related cannot be seen from the material. These names are clearly linked, however, throughout the Districts of Kiambu, Fort Hall, Nyeri, and perhaps Ndia and Kichugu; but they do not seem to have spread into Embu. In some of the lists of names (e.g. Hobley's) the earliest names are those of generation-sets.

Each group of boys (and/or girls) circumcised together acquires their own name; during the years following they meet other such named groups in competitive dancing displays; the name of the group which acquires most honour becomes the name of the set as a whole, and after some time the initial names of the smaller groups are forgotten. Girls' *marika* carry the same name as the boys', but when girls are circumcised during a *muhingo* they acquire a name for their own set. A sub-set consists of

[162] Hobley, 1938, p. 212.
[163] An elder of the highest grade in Hobley's classification.
[164] Hobley, 1938, p. 212. Elsewhere he mentions "Succession ceremonies for an elder's eldest son" (p. 117).
[165] Tate, 1910, p. 238; Stigand, 1913, p. 243.
[166] Lambert, 1956, p. 135.

all the youths circumcised within the year, irrespective of clan or district affiliation. "Men circumcised at the same time stand in the very closest relationship to each other. When a man of the same age-group injures another it is a serious magico-religious offence. They are like blood brothers; they must not do any wrong to each other. It ranks with an injury done to a member of one's own family."[167] Members of the same age-set refer to each other's wives by the same terms as to their own: a visiting age-mate is given access to one of a man's wives for the night, the choice being made by the wives concerned. But those initiated "in the same hut" are regarded as brothers and sisters and sexual relations are forbidden between them. Age-mates help each other in corporate work, payment of fines and avenging of insults.

Sets are thought of in terms of descent. Kinship terminology is used between members of the same circumcision year and especially between members circumcised at the same place and time under the care of the same circumcision-father. These "segments" are given their own name, sometimes the name of a sub-set which has distinguished itself, sometimes a new name. Variation exists in the different parts of Kikuyu country in the duration of the open and closed period and consequently in the length of life of each age-set or segment.[168] This may explain the confusion on this subject which is apparent in the literature.

The circumcision years formed before one *muhingo*, form one age-set. After the reopening of the circumcision a new group of circumcision years constitute a junior age-set. The importance of seniority is stressed, the senior age-set always taking precedence over the junior. The age-sets compose the age grade of the warriors, the *aanake*, although in the senior age-set some members may already have become *athuuri, wa mburi imwe* or *kamatimu*. Each age-set of warriors is thus divided into circumcision-years, for which in the literature the words "regiment" has been used.[169]

After initiation the youth becomes a warrior and a member of the *njama ya aanake a muumo* ("council" of junior warriors); about 6 years later he becomes a senior warrior and a member of the *njama ya ita* (war council).[170]

Age-sets of warriors are based on the district—the territorial unit on which the elders' grades are based. Regiments are therefore not formed according to any component territorial sections of the district, but the entire *njama ya aanake a muumo* is stratified according to the yearly age-sets of its members. Each regiment within the warrior grade "had its village, district and national leaders" (*athamaki a rika*).[171] This would point to a territorial segmentation of the regiment.

From Kenyatta's account it seems that decisions in war were made by the members of the *njama ya ita*. At its head was a *mundu mugo wa ita* (war magician), and he also mentions an official called *muthamaki wa bururi* (the high councillor or chief of the district) but says nothing of his status or duties. The *mundu mugo wa ita* is presumably the "witch doctor" mentioned by Bugeau, who determined when and where attacks were to be made.[172]

In actual warfare raids were led by three leaders, the *athigani*, chosen by medicine men for their personal qualities, and who received a disproportionately large share of the booty. There were also the *ngerewani*, or scouts, and the *atungati*, the actual combatants. Tactics were decided by the *gitungati kia ita cia ngorano*.[173] In times of peace the warrior-age-sets took part in herding and other general occupations, and in physical exercises to keep them in training; they also kept order in markets.[174]

[167] Kenyatta, 1938, pp. 2, 115.

[168] Lambert, 1956, pp. 8 ff.

[169] Kenyatta, 1938, p. 205.

[170] Kenyatta, 1938, pp. 198–200.

[171] Kenyatta, 1938, p. 200. The extent to which they exerted leadership is not yet known. See also Orde-Browne, 1925, pp. 52–3.

[172] Kenyatta, 1938, pp. 205–6; Bugeau, 1943, p. 199.

[173] C. Dundas, 1915, p. 237; Hobley, 1938, pp. 244–5; Bugeau, 1943, pp. 197–204, gives a good description of a raid.

[174] Kenyatta, 1938, pp. 207–8; Cagnolo, 1933, pp. 7, 44, 103–4; Bugeau, 1943, p. 191; von Höhnel, 1894, I, 293.

Cagnolo says that the "old bachelors" had a *njama ya ndundu* which appeared to have some control over warrior activities.[175]

Girls' age-sets took part in ordinary occupations and in preparation for marriage.[176]

In some parts of Kikuyu segments followed an alternating system of left- and right-handedness[177] but more data are needed to study the extent of the institution and its significance.

THE GENERATION-SET SYSTEM

It has been claimed in the literature that age-sets were grouped into generation-sets, which "ruled" the country for a period of 20–30 years. More information is still needed on the subject but it is likely that although the ruling generation handed over its office to the incoming generation about the time that two age-sets had been formed, the generation-set system was a different institution from that of the age-sets. Present information suggests that the generation-set system grouped male Kikuyu into named (cyclical or linear) moieties in which a man was recruited in the set opposite his father and in the same, but junior, set as his grandfather. If a man belonged to the generation set Maina, his son would belong to Mwangi, his grandson would be again Maina and his great-grandson again Mwangi. It is also likely that Maina/Mwangi are generic names and that each generation set had its own name according to a fixed cycle of names. However, sources are still conflicting and it is possible that wide variations existed between the different areas of Kikuyu country.[178]

The generation-set system regulated access to power throughout the institution of Kikuyu society, throughout the age-grades as well as the age-sets. Men could move up and down in the system on the payment of fees and thus occupy positions which might otherwise have been barred to them.

Within the lineage a man's position within the *mbari* might lead him to seek corresponding status within the generation-set system. Whether the generation-set system was still in actual operation in all institutions and in all parts of Kikuyu country is a matter for research. There are some indications that the large-scale movement and the expansion of the population in the last part of the 18th and 19th centuries put the system under strain.

According to Dundas, when the junior generation-set had taken over the "rulership" of the community the retiring generation-set withdrew from its religious and other public duties. Persons of all ages, except children, took part in the *ituika* at which their generation-set either took over, or handed over, its duties; thus "if a young man belongs to a senior generation (set) which retires before he has attained an age at which he could take part in the common sacrifices, he will be for ever excluded from the exercise of such priestly functions."[179]

Generation-sets were thought of in terms of descent and kinship terminology was used between them and could be used within one set.

The handing over of office from one generation-set to the next occurred at a solemn and still largely secret ceremony, the *ituika* ceremony.[180] The ceremony took years to complete all over Kikuyu country, and the last complete ceremony probably took place between 1890 and 1903. The ceremony started in the early thirties was never completed, but years before the aspiring generation-set had started to pay the fees required from them.[181] The colonial government prohibited the completion

[175] Cagnolo, 1933, p. 98.

[176] Cagnolo, 1933, pp. 104–5.

[177] Lambert, 1956, pp. 10, 11, who has a detailed and important account of a number of the local variations in age-set formation.

[178] Lambert, 1956, has here again the most extensive data, pp. 40–52, 137.

[179] C. Dundas, 1915, pp. 246–7.

[180] Kenyatta, 1938, p. 187 states that *ituika* is derived from the word *-tuika*, which means "to break away from". His is the most extensive description of the ceremony and its implications.

[181] Cagnolo, 1933, p. 121.

of the ceremony.[182] Details of the ceremony are not yet clear, neither is its organization. Routledge's account[183] was written under the impression that the ceremony was a form of snake worship, while Kenyatta[184] interprets it as a democratic revolution against the tyranny of King Gikuyu. He describes the first ceremony of *ituika* as the charter for Kikuyu society made up at the time according to tribal legend. Hobley states that there were eight "officiating priests" of the festival, but it is not clear from his account how these men were chosen; all were elders of *ukuru* (or *maturanguru*).[185] Leaders of each *mbari* had to attend the ceremony.[186] More information is still needed.

Kinship System

For a proper understanding of the Kikuyu view of kin, reference must be made to some aspects of their world view. The Kikuyu conceive of individuals, institutions and the people as a whole, as they are living in the present, embodying the past as well as the future. The living male person is his grandfather, he is also his grandson. The generation-set in office is the generation-set alternating above, as well as the as-yet unformed set alternating below. A woman giving birth to her children thus brings forth her parents, so does a generation-set give birth to the next, which is its own parent set. The thought of giving birth, *guciaruu*, as the means by which the present re-creates the past and the future leads to the view of people and institutions as units in descent in which people are kin.[187]

Thus kinship terminology is not only used between relatives through blood and marriage, but also within and between circumcision years, age-sets and generation-sets, as they group people in particular kin-groups. Any "adoption" of one person by another creates kinship, with consequent use of kinship terminology (see the section on land tenure and *mbari*). Purchase and selling of land creates in many instances kinship between the families involved and requires the proper terminology. In the last instance the brotherhood of all Kikuyu is formulated in their joint ancestry and effected through their joint rights within ancestral territory; this general, basic kinship may also lead to the use of kin terms.

A basic range of about 17 terms is used within the confines of lineage and affinal relationships; descriptive terminology is added to indicate whether speaker and person(s) addressed or described belong to the same lineage, the position of each within the lineage, social or physical age, and sex.

Of these 17 terms about 11 can be used in the wider kinship system, the rights and duties involved varying with the setting in which the terms are used. There is a difference in terminology between various parts of Kikuyu country. Cagnolo, who mainly collected information in the northern parts, gives some of the terminology used there[188]; Kenyatta gives an interesting description of a number of the terms and behaviour associated with the specific relationship[189]; Tate gives a list of kinship terms.[190]

Political Organization of the Northern Tribes

The published material on the Meru and Embu groups is unsatisfactory. By far the best account is that by Lambert[191]; others are by Orde-Browne and Bernardi.[192] Their social organization is similar in the main to that of the Kikuyu proper, although different terms are used for many of the groups.

[182] Kenyatta, 1938, p. 196.
[183] Routledge, 1910, pp. 237–8.
[184] Kenyatta, 1938, pp. 190–4.
[185] Hobley, 1938, pp. 93–6.
[186] The following are the most important accounts of our knowledge up to date: Cagnolo, 1933, pp. 121–4; Hobley, 1938, pp. 93–6; C. Dundas, 1915, pp. 245–6; Kenyatta, 1938, pp. 186 ff; Lambert, 1956, p. 58–65.
[187] Leakey, 1952, p. 31 ff.
[188] Cagnolo, 1933, pp. 210–11.
[189] Kenyatta, 1938, pp. 9–18.
[190] Tate, 1911, pp. 291–3.
[191] Lambert, 1947, 1956.
[192] Orde-Browne, 1925; Bernardi, 1959.

The Meru sub-tribes appear to have some form of moiety—or dual—organization; membership is inherited patrilineally. The position is somewhat obscure.[193]

Details of the clan and lineage system are also confused. The word *mwiriga* (pl. *miiriga*) is used by Bernardi for "clan", "sub-clan" and "lineage". The clan is said by him to be exogamous, but "exogamy . . . may be enforced only between the sub-clans or the lineages".[194] Other writers say that the *miiriga* are exogamous and totemic. It is probably best to say that the sub-clans are the exogamous units, thus bringing them into line with the Kikuyu sub-clans: it might indeed be that exogamy is the main criterion of the sub-clan. Various observers give names of *miiriga*, but few coincide; more information is needed.[195]

The Meru clans are divided into three groupings, known as Njiru (the black people), Njeru (the white people) and Ntune (the red people). The origin of these names is given in tradition that when crossing a river into their present home the black clans crossed at night, the red at sunrise and the white in daylight.[196]

The Meru have a system of age-sets based on initiation. Age-sets over a period of from ten to fifteen years are grouped into generation-sets (*nthuki*). Lambert states that "the whole population is grouped into two divisions whose generation periods overlap, so that the taking over occurs at a different date in each. . . . Normally a man belongs to the filial generation of his father's generation and each succeeding generation is the equivalent, or the repetition, of its grandfather generation. The sons of a man in one division, however, could sometimes be transferred into the other".[197] At any one time there are five generation-sets in existence, comprising the age-grades of the Aged, the Old Men, the Ruling Set, the Young Married Men, and the Warriors. When a new set is formed the present ruling set hands over to the succeeding set at the *ntuiko* ceremony. Some of the older warriors remain such for a few years after marriage, until the next *ntuiko*. Generations thus alternate as ruling and non-ruling divisions. The system may be seen in the following diagram[198]:

Division I		Division II
A	Aged	
	Old men	B
C	Ruling set	
	Young married men	D
E	Warriors	
	at the next *ntuiko* the arrangement will become	
	Aged	B
C	Old men	
	Ruling set	D
E	Young married men	
	Warriors	F

According to Lambert, no law is binding beyond the term of office of the set which has passed it, so that after an *ntuiko* the law must be reiterated by the new ruling set. "There is consequently a customary liaison between the two divisions and in practice a new law is only promulgated after consultation and agreement between

[193] Bernardi, 1959, pp. 9–11; Lambert, 1947, pp. 3–4; Orde-Browne, 1925, pp. 39–40; Maxwell Report, 1929, Appendix, pp. 23–4.

[194] Bernardi, 1959, 11 ff.

[195] Barnardi, 1959, pp. 11 ff.; Hobley, 1910, p. 156 f.; Maxwell Report, 1929, p. 29; Holding, 1942, p. 59; Laughton, 1944, p. 2; Lambert, 1950, p. 10; C. Dundas, 1915, pp. 238, 240, 299; Champion, 1912, p. 84, pp. 88–9.

[196] The fullest account is Bernardi, 1959, pp. 52 ff.; see also the analysis by Needham, 1960.

[197] Lambert, 1956. p. 42.

[198] Diagram from Lambert, 1950. See also Lambert, 1947, p. 4; 1956, pp. 23 ff., p. 42 f., pp. 47 ff.; Bernardi, 1959, pp. 20 ff.; Holding, 1952, pp. 59 ff.

Details of the *ntuiko* are given by Bernardi, 1959, pp. 22 ff., 112 ff.; Lambert, 1956, pp. 62 ff.

the two. This is effected by reference to the lodges (*biama*)."[199] There are three lodges or councils. The lowest is that of the warriors, responsible for warriors' discipline, warfare and political executive duties. The next council is the *kiama* to which all married men belong, and the senior council is the *njuri ya kiama*, which is the council responsible for judicial activities. Lambert states that "every sort and size of territorial unit larger than a multiple extended family is governed by a member of the *njuri* who belongs to it".[200] Another way of expressing this would seem to be that the heads of the territorial units are by virtue of that status members of the *njuri*, as in the Kikuyu system. Much weight is given to *agambi* (sing. *mugambi*), influential leaders chosen for their wisdom as well as genealogical position.[201]

An important judicial role is also played by the sacred functionary known as the *mugwe*, whose powers are largely prophetic and concerned with ritual pollution and purification. The only published account of the *mugwe*, who is clearly of great importance in the traditional political system of the Meru, is by Bernardi.[202]

There is a related system of age- and generation-sets for women.[203] And Lambert states that the Meru also place importance on the pre-initiation sets for both boys and girls.[204]

Law and Legal Procedure

There is a considerable amount of information as to Kikuyu and Tharaka law and procedure and almost none on those of the other tribes. Unless otherwise stated, this section refers to Kikuyu only, but it may be assumed that a good deal of the information is also applicable to the other tribes.

Traditional Kikuyu law recognizes both private and public delicts. Private delicts, when the dispute is between different *mbari*, are submitted to arbitration by the elders—the *kiama kia athamaki*; judgment is passed by the council, and the injured party is then entitled to compensation. Public delicts also come before the council of elders, who pass judgment and carry out punishment, in the form of either a curse or putting to death. The procedure is similar in both cases; the differences lie in the sanctions involved in the settlement and punishment.

(I) Private Delicts

Private delicts in the indigenous legal system include:

(*a*) *Homicide*

The usual way of dealing with homicide is for the victim's kin to retaliate: if the murderer or one of his close kin is killed the matter is considered settled. If not, the victim's kin lay waste the murderer's fields, and the matter is then brought before the elders for arbitration.[205] Compensation is then payable by the murderer's kin.

Homicide is the same offence in all circumstances. Provocation, self-defence or absence of intention are not accepted as extenuating circumstances.[206] Analogously among the Kikuyu and Tharaka the killing of a man by some property or animal belonging to another (i.e. death caused by the fall of a beehive from a tree) is regarded as homicide. Death need not ensue immediately or within a given period: "it is sufficient that a blow or wound inflicted is ultimately the cause of death, no matter how many years may have elapsed between the two events". The causes of death are usually ascribed to witchcraft or the effects of injury. A post-mortem is often held.[207]

The relationship between the slayer and his victim is important in regard to compensation. No compensation is payable among the Kikuyu and Tharaka for the

[199] Lambert, 1947, pp. 4–5. *Biama* is the plural of *kiama*.
[200] Lambert, 1947, p. 5.
[201] Lambert, 1947, pp. 4–5; 1956, pp. 66–95, 100 ff.; Holding, 1942, pp. 63–65; Bernardi, pp. 24 ff., pp. 138 ff., pp. 150 ff.
[202] Bernardi, 1959, *passim*. See also Needham, 1960.
[203] Holding, 1942, pp. 62–65; Lambert, 1956, pp. 51.
[204] Lambert, 1956, pp. 3 ff., 35.
[205] Kenyatta, 1938, p. 227; Routledge, 1910, p. 219.
[206] C. Dundas, 1915, pp. 263, 264; 1921, p. 239; Kenyatta, 1938, p. 227; Tate, 1910, pp. 241, 248. But Champion states that this is not so among the Tharaka (1912, p. 85).
[207] C. Dundas, 1915, p. 263; also Kenyatta, 1938, p. 228; C. Dundas, 1921, p. 240.

killing of a wife, father, mother, sister, or daughter (except in Ndia, where a bull is payable to the "clan" for patricide, to the father in case of matricide, and to the "clan" for the killing of a man's own son). Half blood-money is payable for the death of a full brother, to another brother, among the Kikuyu; among the Tharaka, only one bull is paid to the "clan" for this offence.[208] Dundas states that half blood-money is payable for the killing of a clansman among the Kikuyu (full blood-money among the Tharaka), while Routledge states that no compensation need be paid for the killing of a clansman in one's own district. Details vary from one part of the country to another. Rules of precedence play an important part in legal deliberations. In cases where the slayer kills a person for whose killing he would normally be compensated, he will pay no compensation.[209]

Killing of or by a "stranger" (a member of another clan or district may be meant) is subject to compensation only if the stranger has been fully adopted by the claimant or if he has entered into blood-brotherhood with a member of the family. In Ndia if a stranger kills anyone his host must always pay full blood-money; among the Tharaka the life of a stranger must be compensated in every case, and the host is responsible for all actions of his guest.[210] The Mwimbi pay blood-money only for the killing of a fellow Mwimbi, none for that of an outsider.[211]

Killing of a cripple should be compensated by payment of full blood-money less any compensation previously paid for the hurt. Full compensation is therefore payable if the cripple has been crippled since birth. The principle is that more than the value of a man's life must never be paid for his person. Half blood-money is payable if a man strikes a corpse or takes part in a fatal fight.[212]

Blood-money for a woman is approximately one-third of that for a man, among the Kikuyu, and this Dundas states corresponds to the average bridewealth; among the Tharaka the amount is the same for either sex.[213]

In addition in all cases of homicide a fine (*ngoima*) is payable to the elders and a goat "for the spear" by which the man was killed: the spear is broken and the goat eaten by the murderer's "tribe".[214]

The greater part of the blood-money is subscribed and received by the respective "clan" of the parties concerned. Routledge states that liability extends to "all members of the clan over a very large district".[215] The persons who share out the blood-money are given as the claimant, the deceased's brothers and their sons, the maternal grandmother, and "the clan"—who "the clan" are is not stated.[216] Another account states that the recipients are the father, if dead, his brother, failing him the maternal uncle, failing him the son. Where it is paid to the father, the "uncle, male cousin or nephew on the mother's side" receive compensation also.[217] In the case of the killing of a married woman the husband is the only recipient, and of an unmarried woman, it would seem, the father.[218]

The compensation is handed over at the *mugiro* ceremony, which includes, besides the actual transfer of blood-money, a ritual appeasement of the ancestors and so a reconciliation of the two clans, which would otherwise be unable to have further

[208] Tate, 1910, p. 239; C. Dundas, 1915, p. 265; 1921, p. 242; Hobley (1938, p. 234) says that no compensation is payable for the killing of a full brother.
[209] C. Dundas, 1915, pp. 265–6; 1921, pp. 241–2; Routledge, 1910, p. 20.
[210] C. Dundas, 1915, p. 267.
[211] Gurney, 1929, p. 206.
[212] C. Dundas, 1915, p. 264; 1921, p. 239.
[213] C. Dundas, 1915, p. 269; 1921, p. 247; Hobley, 1938, p. 234.
[214] Tate, 1910, p. 239.
[215] C. Dundas, 1915, p. 267; 1921, p. 238; Routledge, 1910, p. 20; but see Champion, 1912, p. 85.
[216] C. Dundas, 1915, p. 268.
[217] Tate, 1910, pp. 238–9; Hobley, 1938, p. 232.
[218] C. Dundas, 1915, pp. 269–72. He adds: "It should be remarked that when a native speaks of killing a woman, he . . . contemplates only death in childbirth resulting from illicit intercourse. He cannot conceive that a man should intentionally kill a woman, for this would not be done even in time of war, nor is it likely that a woman should be mixed up in brawls." See also Tate, 1910, p. 239.

social intercourse with one another. There are descriptions of the ceremony by Hobley and Dundas.[219] It is the same for both guilds. Hobley states that in south Kikuyu there were only two persons qualified to perform the ritual, apparently brothers, the sons of a "chief" of the Anjiru clan. Among the Tharaka purification of a homicide must be performed in all cases, or "the murderer will continue to slay friends and foes alike". The killer's weapon is blunted and buried by the elders.

(*b*) *Physical Injury*

No difference is made in the compensation payable for injuries done intentionally or unintentionally, or whether done to a man or a woman.[220] For many injuries the compensation is fixed by custom. For other wounds, Dundas states that one goat is payable for each thorn used in the stitching of the wound, plus one for slaughtering and consumption by the elders and one for the suffering caused. Among the Tharaka if a man injures a girl he must marry her, and if he injures another man's wife "so as to impair her usefulness" he must pay the husband the bridewealth for another wife. Among the Tharaka also if a man is injured on the right arm he receives all the compensation, but if on the left arm, half goes to his mother's family, since "the left arm belongs to the mother's family".[221]

(*c*) *Sexual Offences*

Sexual intimacy short of actual intercourse is permitted between unmarried adolescents; this is known as *nguiko*.[222]

If a girl is made pregnant and dies in childbirth, full compensation for homicide must be paid. Compensation is demanded for causing an unmarried girl to become pregnant: it seems to be the same amount as is deducted from the bridewealth returned to the husband who divorces his wife after she has become pregnant for the first time.[223]

Adultery is a private delict against the husband and requires compensation. The compensation is comparatively small provided the woman stays with her husband and comes to no physical harm.[224] A child conceived by a man other than a woman's husband is a member of the husband's *mbari*.[225]

Rape is a private delict against the woman's guardian whether she is married or unmarried: it is regarded as being of the same degree of seriousness in either case.[226]

It is clear that in sexual offences a distinction is made between offences which affect the husband's sole right of sexual access to his wife, and those which affect her procreative powers and the rights over those powers, which are transferred to the husband's lineage or *mbari* by the transfer of bridewealth. The distinction applies also to unmarried girls.

(*d*) *Divorce*

A woman can return to her father, and her husband cannot restrain her. If she has not borne a child, the bridewealth is returned to her husband and she is free to remarry. If she has children, Dundas states that bridewealth is returned to the husband in part or in full according to the number of children he retains, whereas Routledge states that the bridewealth cannot be returned "under any circumstances".

[219] Hobley, 1938, pp. 230–3; C. Dundas, 1915, pp. 269–71; 1921, pp. 242–3.

[220] C. Dundas, 1915, p. 272; Routledge, 1910, p. 216.

[221] C. Dundas, 1915, pp 273, 280, 282–3: he gives full lists showing compensations due. See also Kenyatta, 1938, p. 229; Routledge, 1910, p. 215; Tate, 1910, pp. 239–41; K. R. Dundas, 2, 1908, p. 181; for Tharaka see C. Dundas, 1915, p. 281; Champion, 1912, pp. 85–6.

[222] See above, p. 33.

[223] C. Dundas, 1915, p. 273; 1921, p. 247; Routledge, 1910, p. 216; Kenyatta, 1938, p. 160; Cagnolo, 1933, p. 114; Phillips, 1945, p. 48; Orde-Browne (1925, pp. 70–1) states that this compensation is taken off the bridewealth if he later marries her.

[224] C. Dundas, 1915, pp. 280, 282–3; Kenyatta, 1938, p. 182; Tate, 1910, p. 242.

[225] C. Dundas, op. cit., p. 275.

[226] C. Dundas, 1915, p. 274; Cagnolo, 1933, p. 156; Tate, 1910, p. 242; Orde-Browne, 1925, p. 71.

If the bridewealth is not returned and the woman has children by another man they belong to her legal husband and he receives compensation for her if she is killed.[227]

A husband can divorce his wife for barrenness, refusal of conjugal rights, witchcraft, theft, desertion or habitual adultery; and a wife may divorce her husband on all these grounds except adultery and also for cruelty and drunkenness.[228] Sexual taboos binding on a wife are given below[229]; whether breaking them is considered grounds for divorce is not stated.

(*e*) *Theft*

Theft is uncommon and is severely dealt with; it is regarded as a wrong done to the individual and not to the community. "The name of thief. . . carries a peculiar stigma with it, and whilst almost every other offence is attributed to circumstances rather than to character, that of theft signifies an unpardonable nature. . . . Practically always when a native commits theft (sic) from another he is taking by force or stealth something which he claims, and this is regarded as a perfectly legitimate procedure",[230] but it seems from Tate that it is only legal if permission has been given by the elders who tried the case and awarded compensation which the guilty party refuses to pay. They sweep a path with sacred leaves "within the sight of the debtor's hut", saying "May the goats be stolen."[231]

The most common form of theft is that of livestock; a man was entitled to kill a thief caught in the act of taking stock without being liable for compensation. The theft of beehives is also regarded as a serious crime.[232]

Routledge gives a list of fines for theft.[233] The Tharaka do not seem to distinguish degrees of theft; a thief pays seven goats, but if he has stolen from a clansman he pays one goat and swears on oath not to repeat the offence.[234]

(*f*) *Debt*

Kenyatta states that cases involving debts arising from land or bridewealth transactions are those most frequently brought before the elders.[235] The commonest land disputes are those concerning boundaries, which in many cases involve payments made when the land was acquired from the Dorobo.[236]

Debts are heritable, and if livestock is concerned the increase is included in the payment.[237]

Dundas states that girls are often given in place of blood-money or for other debts and are supposed to become wives or children of the claimant; but if they wish to marry someone else the claimant has ultimately only the right to the bridewealth paid for them.[238]

(II) PUBLIC DELICTS

(*a*) *Theft*

A man who constantly steals stock, honey or hives would be put to death.[239]

(*b*) *Sorcery*

Sorcery is not regarded as a private delict, and accusations of its practice cannot

[227] Routledge, 1910, p. 217; Tate, 1910, p. 242; Kenyatta, 1938, p. 185; C. Dundas, 1915, pp. 288–9; 1921, p. 262.
[228] Kenyatta, 1938, pp. 183–4; Cagnolo, 1933, pp. 60–1.
[229] See below, p. 60.
[230] C. Dundas, 1915, p. 276.
[231] Tate, 1910, p. 245.
[232] C. Dundas, 1915, pp. 275–6; 1921, p. 233; Tate, 1910, p. 241.
[233] Routledge, 1910, p. 216; also Cagnolo, 1933, p. 156.
[234] C. Dundas, 1915, p. 276.
[235] Kenyatta, 1938, p. 217; Routledge, 1910, p. 125; Orde-Browne, 1925, p. 75.
[236] See below, pp. 48–9.
[237] Tate, 1910, p. 245; C. Dundas, 1915, p. 292.
[238] C. Dundas, 1921, p. 276.
[239] C. Dundas, 1915, p. 275; Kenyatta, 1938, p. 230; Routledge, 1910, p. 216; Cagnolo, 1933, p. 156.

be brought before the elders for arbitration. A persistent sorcerer would be put to death; in Kikuyu sorcerers are usually men, in Tharaka, women.[240]

(III) Legal Procedure

(*a*) *Procedure for Private Delicts*

If a matter cannot be settled by the parties concerned, they agree to submit the case to arbitration by the elders of the units concerned. The elders hear the evidence, which is given by the principals; in Tharaka the principals speak only through proxies.[241] The case is then discussed by all the elders present, and witnesses are questioned. The *ndundu* or "inner council" then retires to consider judgment: the *ndundu* consists of the elders of *ukuru* or senior elders present, but anyone with a direct or indirect interest in the case is excluded.[242]

During the *ndundu*'s retirement the animals paid in as "elders' fees" are killed and roasted by the *kamatimo* elders. The galls are broken by the *ndundu* who use them to curse any of those concerned in the case who lie. The meat is then eaten, the portions being distributed according to rank. The findings are then announced. Two elders are appointed to see that the judgment is carried out by the parties concerned. The guilty party is given two days in which to pay the debt. If one of the parties does not agree with the judgment, appeal may be made and the case re-heard, according to Kenyatta, but Tate states that under the indigenous system there was no appeal from the decision of the elders.[243]

The present system is rather different, although it is based on the indigenous procedure.[244]

In all cases of compensation and fine, the terms used are: *ngoima*, the "court fees" paid to the elders arbitrating in the case; they are often required for purification rites[245]; *ngaita*, compensation paid to the injured party, in addition to the compensation proper, to "assist his recovery" (usually one goat[246]; *rukwaro*, a piece of goat-skin worn on the wrist of the injured party in a case involving physical injury. It is placed on the wrist by the elders, who sacrifice the goat first. But a *rukwaro* is also worn by an offender who has broken a taboo or by a person who has taken various oaths or made various sacrifices.[247] It is clearly worn by people who are in, or have just come out of, a state of ritual danger.

In the arbitration procedure concerned with private delicts there is no organized force as sanction behind the elders and their decisions. When judgment is passed the party in whose favour it is given may receive compensation, but no organized force is employed to ensure that he is paid. However, Kenyatta states that in cases involving property, "the property involved in the judgment was not given to the plaintiffs directly, but was passed through the hands of the appointed elders who acted on behalf of the whole *kiama*. If the claim was not settled the plaintiff could not go directly to the defendant, his proper channel was through the elders in charge of the case."[248] This procedure points to the bringing into action of other sanctions by the elders to ensure that their judgment is acted upon. These sanctions are expressed in oaths and curses.

Both parties in the case and the elders had to take oaths before the beginning of a case, the former to give true evidence and the latter to give unbiased judgment. Dundas states that "oaths differ from ordeals in that they are not intended merely

[240] C. Dundas, 1915, pp. 277–8; Kenyatta, 1938, p. 230.

[241] Champion, 1912, p. 87.

[242] Kenyatta, 1938, pp. 219–21; C. Dundas, 1915, pp. 250, 251; Routledge, 1910, pp. 209–12; Cagnolo, 1933, pp. 149–50; Tate, 1910, p. 253; 1911, p. 295; Phillips, 1945, p. 38; Champion, 1912, p. 87.

[243] Kenyatta, 1938, pp. 221–3; Cagnolo, 1933, p. 150; Tate, 1910, pp. 245, 253; 1911, p. 295.

[244] See Hobley, 1938, pp. 216–19, 306–15; Phillips, 1945, pp. 36 ff.; Hailey, 1950, Part I, chap. II; Middleton, 1965.

[245] C. Dundas, 1915, p. 257; also Routledge, 1910, p. 218.

[246] Tate, 1910, p. 242.

[247] C. Dundas, 1915, p. 263; 1921, p. 243; Tate, 1910, pp. 239, 242, 244, 249.

[248] Kenyatta, 1938, p. 222; the elders referred to are the two elders appointed to see the judgment carried out.

to betray the guilt of a man who will thereafter be dealt with; they signify, rather, that the matter is thenceforth beyond the sphere of human justice, and that the guilt as well as its penalty is left to divine judgment''.[249] The form that oaths and ordeals take may often be the same. The oaths described below indicate the taker's innocence, and thus his willingness to accept the result of arbitration. An oath also has the function, of course, of strengthening the belief in the powers and divine guidance of the elders.

There are three main kinds of oaths: they are always taken by the accused alone or by him in the first instance.[250]

The oath called *muuma* (which is also the word used for "ordeal") is generally taken in minor disputes. The person taking the oath licks a brushful of the contents of a lamb's stomach mixed with sacred herbs, and swears on it not to lie. If abused the oath will take effect in three seasons.[251]

The oath called *kuringa thenge* ("to swear by killing a ram") is more serious. The parties concerned, who must all be males, break the limbs of a ram, saying that their own limbs should be broken also if they lie. Hobley states that the ceremony can be performed only by members of certain clans; it is uncertain whether "perform" means to take or to administer the oath. A similar oath is found among the Northern tribes.[252]

The third and most serious form of oath, taken in cases of murder, sorcery and theft, is that taken on a *githathi*, an object having great power, usually made of stone or clay and kept in secret by a member of the Aithaga clan; the writers who have seen a *githathi* all say that it has seven holes in it, seven being a sacred number. Tate says that the oath made on it is repeated for seven days, in a temporary grass hut built in the bush. The offender who takes the oath is ritually unclean, since at the end of seven days he is shaved and wears the *rukwaro* wristlet; the elders who administer the oath must not have sexual intercourse for three months.[253]

Hobley mentions an oath taken by members of the Kikuyu guild only on certain sacred blue beads.[254] Cagnolo writes that a suspected sorcerer may have to swear his innocence on the corpse of the victim.[255]

Ordeals are common, and are closely connected with oaths. They include licking a red-hot knife, having medicine put in the eyelid, taking poison, and carrying fire. They are all administered by a medicine man (*mundu mugo*) and among the Northern tribes at any rate can be undergone by proxy.[256]

Oaths and ordeals must be administered in the presence of the elders, and oaths, as distinct from ordeals, are administered by the elders themselves. Oaths are said to be "bad", which signifies that they are connected with the "spirits". Refusal to submit to an oath or ordeal is regarded as proof of guilt, and a suspected person will often demand to be allowed to disprove suspicion by the performance of such a test.[257]

Elders will curse a man if he delays to answer a court summons, or if he refuses to pay the fees or to carry out the decisions of the council.[258]

[249] C. Dundas, 1915, pp. 255–6; Kenyatta, 1938, p. 223.

[250] C. Dundas, 1921, p. 227.

[251] Kenyatta, 1938, pp. 223–4; Tate, 1910, pp. 248–50; C. Dundas, 1915, p. 254; Phillips, 1945, p. 45.

[252] Kenyatta, 1938, p. 224; Cagnolo, 1933, p. 152; Tate, 1910, pp. 244, 248, 251; Hobley, 2, 1910, pp. 142–3; C. Dundas, 1915, p. 255; Orde-Browne, 1925, pp. 198–9.

[253] Tate, 1910, pp. 244, 248–9; 1918, pp. 263–4; Routledge, 1910, pp. 273–5; Hobley, 2, 1910, pp. 139–42; C. Dundas, 1915, p. 253; 1921, pp. 229–30; Phillips, 1945, p. 45, refers to it as the *Jiwe* oath (*jiwe* is the Swahili for stone).

[254] Hobley, 1938, pp. 241–3.

[255] Cagnolo, 1933, p. 158.

[256] Routledge, 1910, pp. 212–13; Cagnolo, 1933, pp. 150–1; C. Dundas, 1915, pp. 253–6; Crawford, 1909, p. 55; Orde-Browne, 1925, pp. 196–8; Gurney, 1924, p. 205.

[257] See C. Dundas, 1915, pp. 256–7.

[258] Tate, 1910, p. 254; C. Dundas, 1915, pp. 257–8; Tate, 1911, p. 295; Orde-Browne, 1925, p. 56.

Suicide is stated to be common among the Kikuyu. It seems to be designed to bring public reprobation and powerful mystical sanctions to bear on others.[259]

(*b*) *Procedure for Public Delicts*

Among the Kikuyu a persistent offender guilty of private or public delicts would be put to death; this process is carried out by *muingi*, and is comparable with the Kamba *king'oli*. The term is often translated as "lynching", but this is inaccurate: Dundas states that action taken by *muingi* includes almost every form of legal sanction used by recognized authority, and nowadays is often applied to imprisonment and other measures taken by the central administration.[260]

In the milder form of action taken by *muingi* the offender would be expelled from the district and his homestead destroyed. In no such case was violence to the man himself permitted, and he could claim compensation for personal injury. It was usual to warn him by sending him a firestick.[261]

Death was only inflicted on persistent evil-doers. The telling point was the frequency of the crime, rather than its gravity. Only those guilty of persistent theft or sorcery were put to death. The elders consulted and took evidence on the *githathi* oath. His nearest relative was asked to give consent to the man's death; if he refused it, sentence could not be carried out, but he had to swear by *githathi* that if the offences were repeated he would not withhold his consent to the sentence. When the offender was killed the matter was never mentioned afterwards, and no one could ask who had killed him. No compensation was payable.[262]

Dundas states that the victim was put to death by strangulation by his "nearest relative". Kenyatta states that a convicted sorcerer was burnt, the fire being put to the pyre by his nearest kinsman. Cagnolo states that the same fate may await thieves. A sorcerer might also be killed by crucifixion at a crossroads, but this was rare. Cagnolo says that a thief might be crucified on an ant-hill, killed by stoning or drowned. After the execution of a sorcerer a purification ceremony for the assembled public was performed at a sacred tree.[263]

Dundas adds that "procedure in the death sentence is of great importance, as any omission would deprive it of its essential grounds for justification."[264]

Among the Tharaka, in the same circumstances, a man was publicly beaten, very severely but not so as to cause death. The victim was gagged so that he could not utter curses.[265]

INHERITANCE AND SUCCESSION

Distinction must be made between the inheritance of cultivated land and other property, and that of authority. With regard to the first the principle is that property shall be divided among the sons so that each son will share in the property associated with his mother and her hut;[266] this includes cultivated land, livestock and movable property. Authority, with which is associated the care of widows and daughters, and the control of unallotted land, is connected with the headship of the group; it will be passed to the succeeding head or, if fission occurs, to the heads of the resulting segments. Inheritance is thus a process which takes place in the elementary or polygynous family; succession takes place at the level both of the elementary or polygynous family and that of the *mbari*.

[259] Beech, 2, 1913, pp. 56–7, Routledge, 1910, p. 248.

[260] C. Dundas, 1915, pp. 258–61; also Radcliffe-Brown, 1933, pp. 205–6.

[261] C. Dundas, 1915, p. 258. There may be some confusion here between the process of *muingi* carried out by the district elders and ostracism by the clan; the man could then no longer take part in dances or beer-parties, nor could he appeal to the (district) elders if wronged. (Cagnolo, 1933, p. 155).

[262] C. Dundas, 1915, pp. 258–9; 1921, p. 234.

[263] C. Dundas, 1915, p. 259; Kenyatta, 1938, pp. 304–5; Cagnolo, 1933, pp. 156–7; Hobley, 1938, pp. 237–8; Routledge, 1910, p. 216.

[264] C. Dundas, 1915, p. 259.

[265] C. Dundas, 1921, p. 254.

[266] Hobley, 1938, p. 100; Tate, 1910, p. 247.

Sons have rights in all land cultivated by their mother. They take over their plots as they need them, that is, as they marry. This process takes place both during the father's lifetime and after his death. Each widow retains her portion of the plot, but surrenders part to her daughters-in-law as her sons marry.[267]

If the eldest son of any wife is a minor at the time of his father's death, a brother of the deceased is appointed as trustee until the son is of age to take over the property: this is regarded as being married. If there is no son, the property goes to the deceased's senior full brother, or failing a full brother to the senior half-brother, or to the surviving heir of either of these.[268] Beech says that if one wife has no son, she will use her property until her death, then it will pass to the sons of another wife.[269] Since the Kikuyu practise leviratic marriage (or if a widow goes elsewhere to have sons in concubinage they belong to the dead man), it is possible that this property will pass to the sons born after the husband's death. If a widow is too old to have a child, she may acquire a girl with her deceased husband's property, and this girl (who is called his "wife") cohabits with a clansman of the dead man. Her male children become his heirs.[270]

Dundas gives the order of inheritance as son, father, brother, uncle, and, failing these, the "clan"; daughters cannot inherit property: if there are only female children the brother inherits as he would normally do if there were no sons.[271]

Some writers state that division of chattels may be made by bequest or will. Dundas states that among the Kikuyu inheritance by will is so much the rule that no fixed custom as to distribution can be laid down, but that "the father's power to make a will may be said to be confined to bequeathing his property to his immediate heirs only, so that it is in practice only the distribution which he decides". Phillips states that movable property may be bequeathed by will, but "if the deceased has immovable property he cannot wrong his sons and will it away to one son only, as every son is entitled to his portion".[272] We may see from this statement the difference between land and movable property: the latter is regarded as the personal possession of the individual owner, due perhaps to his having acquired it by his own labour. Presumably, certain livestock would be excluded as belonging to the whole family, but the material is very slight on this point. It would also seem likely that it is the distribution of the various pieces of property which is decided by will, rather than the naming of successors to the status of the deceased.[273]

Hobley mentions that a dying man can put an entail on a piece of property by a curse (*kirumi*); *kirumi* can also refer to a dying curse directed against a particular person. It is really a form of ritual uncleanness and can only be removed from a person by the elders of *ukuru*; it can never be removed from property.[274] Beech states that a son may be disinherited by his father for misdemeanour: if he is an only son, property may pass "to a friend".[275]

The rules of inheritance of cultivated land and movable property are applicable within the elementary and polygynous family, whereas rules of succession operate within the *mbari*. Whereas cultivated land and property are redistributed throughout the family group at the death of its head, succession to his status and authority go to the succeeding head of the group, or to the heads of the resulting segments if fission takes place. If the head is in the relationship of father to the heads of the various component families in the *mbari* there will also be a redistribution of cul-

[267] Barlow, 1932, p. 63.

[268] Routledge, 1910, p. 145; C. Dundas, 1915, p. 295; Beech, 1917, p. 59; C. Dundas, 1921, p. 267; Tate, 1910, p. 247; Routledge adds that the will of the deceased decides whether the property shall pass to one or to all the brothers.

[269] Beech, 1917, p. 59.

[270] C. Dundas, 1915, p. 295; also, 1921, p. 267.

[271] C. Dundas, 1915, p. 294; 1921, p. 268; Beech, 1917, pp. 56, 136; Barlow, 1932, p. 63.

[272] C. Dundas, 1915, p. 294; Phillips, 1945, p. 48; also Routledge, 1940, p. 143; Barlow, 1932, p. 63.

[273] See Phillips, 1945, p. 68; Cagnolo, 1933, p. 31.

[274] Hobley, 1938, pp. 143–52; 1911, pp. 406–31; also Kenyatta, 1938, p. 114.

[275] Beech, 1917, p. 138.

tivated land and movable property throughout the whole group; if he is their brother, the redistribution will be within his own segment only. Thus the senior member of the family will inherit his father's authority, but no disproportionate share of the property.[276]

With succession to the father's authority goes the care of his widows and unmarried daughters. The senior wife may not remarry; she is inherited by the husband's brother or may live with a mate (*mwendia ruhiu*).[277] The younger wives may be inherited by the deceased younger brothers or by his sons.[278] A man may not inherit the wife of his deceased son, nor the widow of a younger brother, because he stands in the relation of father to her.[279] Tate states that if a widow has no brother-in-law younger than her husband, nor a stepson to inherit her, "she passes to a man of her own clan".[280] No mention is made of return to bridewealth in this case. Leakey states that the future of a widow is connected with the inheritance of property. The widow of a man who leaves no brother, half-brother or son, and who does not leave his property to a more distant agnatic relative, takes a lover so as to bear to her late husband a son who can inherit the property. If the widow is past child-bearing age she is expected to "marry" a wife and to give bridewealth for her in the usual way. The marriage is consummated by ceremonial sexual intercourse with a man of the late husband's age-set, but later the wife lives with a man of her own choice. This man has no rights over her children or her property, since these belong to her legal "husband", the widow.[281] Children a widow bears after her husband's death belong to his line. A widow must be purified before going to another man.[282]

The deceased's brother succeeds to the paternal care of his unmarried daughters and receives the bridewealth given for them.[283]

Kikuyu Land Tenure

For a proper understanding of Kikuyu land tenure reference must first be made to the system of beliefs which govern the relationship between the people and their land. To the Kikuyu land is not just the economic asset of a group but it enshrines their very existence. The common right of all Kikuyu in the ancestral land as children of Gikuyu and Muumbi makes them all into members of the *mbari* of Gikuyu in which they are all brothers to each other; they are not only children of Muumbi but also children of this ancestral land which is their father and mother. The land is Kikuyu past since it is where the ancestors are and thus stands for the ancestors themselves; it is Kikuyu present because living people are these ancestors and it is Kikuyu future because in them the future (their grandchildren) is already there. The same system of thought which determines the relations between general Kikuyu and their mythological ancestral property governs the relationship within specific Kikuyu *mbari*. A *mbari* cannot be thought of apart from its land: in many respects the *mbari* is its land, its *githaka*. It is thus that kinship not only exists between all Kikuyu but specifically between members belonging to the same *mbari* or between people who have bought and sold land to each other so that kinship terminology can be used between them.

The same system of belief sheds light on the acquisition of land in Kiambu by the Kikuyu, probably since the late 17th century; the land and its original owners, the Dorobo, had to be made, through adoption, into Kikuyu land and Kikuyu before actual sales could be made.

[276] C. Dundas, 1915, p. 300; also Hobley, 2, 1910, p. 139; Beech, 1917, p. 138.

[277] C. Dundas, 1915, pp. 287, 301; 1921, p. 259; Orde-Browne, 1925, p. 72; Tate, 1910, pp 246–7.

[278] Routledge, 1910, p. 143; Beech, 1917, p. 143; C. Dundas, 1915, pp. 287, 301; Tate, 1910, p. 246.

[279] C. Dundas, 1921, p. 259; also 1915, pp. 287, 301.

[280] Tate, 1910, p. 246.

[281] Leakey, unpublished MS.

[282] Cagnolo, 1933, pp. 115–16; he gives a description of the purification.

[283] Routledge, 1910, p. 145.

The Kikuyu are often quoted as providing an example of the outright sale of and under indigenous conditions. The Maxwell Report states that "there are *ithaka* n the Kiambu District which were bought by one group of Kikuyu from another, or by one individual from another, before the coming of the Europeans, and the ransaction was in each case an outright sale of land."[284] The essence of sale in this sense is that ownership of the land is transferred, and not merely limited rights over t; there is no condition of redemption, and the land may be disposed of by the purchaser on his own authority and inherited by his own heirs alone. Lambert suggests that the original transactions between Kikuyu and Dorobo, on which most of the evidence for indigenous land-sale rests, were of the *muguri* type, but that the Dorobo died out and were absorbed without redemption taking place.

The Kenya Land Commission attempted to make a decision on the question of ndigenous outright sale of land, it being one of their principal points of enquiry, but could not come to a decision.

Leakey has always maintained that, after adoption, these sales definitely did take place and were outright transfer of ownership.[285] Present-day knowledge tends to confirm this view.

Lambert gives a description of the solemn adoption ceremony which preceded the sale in Kiambu.[286] In Fort Hall and probably in Nyeri a slightly different system occurred. Sales in Fort Hall were not outright, but redeemable; in Nyeri occupation and ownership were by first clearance, while details of sales are still nsufficiently known. Kenyatta states that the two types of claim to a piece of land, by clearing or by purchase from the Dorobo, are the same in principle; the Dorobo's rights based on first clearing were purchased.[287]

The Kikuyu system of land tenure is often referred to as "the *githaka* system". The Maxwell Report states: "We have defined *githaka* as the Kikuyu unit of land tenure. A *githaka* today may consist of entirely bush or forest land, entirely cultivated land or some of each. Its original sense was bushland but it has come to have the above technical sense."[288]

The head of each *mbari* on its *githaka* in his role as controller of the group's land s called *muramati* (pl. *aramati*), as also is the head of a segment of the *mbari* living on a territorially district *githaka*. The chief duty of the *muramati* is to control the allocation and use of the land. He need not be the most senior member of the group concerned, and he has no more cultivation or building rights than his brothers. He has the power to adjust the allotment of holdings within the *mbari* and to admit or refuse tenants.[289] A *mbari* has only one head, but may have several *aramati*.

The *muramati* allocates land to the *mbari* segments; the principles on which the allotment is made are those of need and of matri-segmentation: that is to say, the founders of the component families of the *mbari* inherited their plots of land from their mother "houses" and any resulting maldistribution is corrected by the *muramati* when a family is short of land. Land allotted includes arable, grazing, forest and other "reserved" land.

Within the household the "houses" of the various wives are kept in a large measure distinct; each wife has her own gardens, and the goats which she buys with their produce are settled on her "house" as a separate inheritance for her sons, and for her own support in widowhood. The gardens of a household are nearly always scattered, either because the householder likes to cultivate on different types of soil, or because his wives like to have their gardens separate, or because he is a rightholder on more than one *githaka*. Kenyatta states that each wife is given several

[284] Maxwell Report, 1929, p. 70; also Beech, 1917, pp. 55, 6; Barlow, 1932, p. 62; Hobley, 1910, p. 137.

[285] Leakey, 1956, p. 3 ff.

[286] Lambert, 1950.

[287] C. Dundas, 1915, p. 297; 1921, p. 272; Maxwell Report, 1929, p. 6; Hobley, 1938, p. 146; Kenyatta, 1938, p. 27.

[288] Maxwell Report, 1929, p. 69. See also Barlow, 1932, p. 57, Liversage, 1945, p. 4. The plural of *githaka* is *ithaka*.

[289] Maxwell Report, 1929, Appendix, p. 37; also Report, p. 9; Kenyatta, 1938, p. 33.

scattered plots, the acreage being "according to her capacity of cultivation". The wife calls her plots *migunda* or *thanju* and refers to the rest of the family land as *githaka*.[290]

If a member of the *mbari* wishes to clear a piece of unallotted land within the boundaries of the *githaka* he may do so, "providing that there was no taboo or custom prohibiting cultivation on this particular piece of land".[291] In short, individual members of a domestic family (and so in time the domestic families themselves as corporate groups) acquire their holdings on the basis of descent from the father through the mother, by the use of a portion of her part of the *githaka*; this portion comes under their control by its use being passed by the mother to her daughters-in-law.

Under the Kikuyu system, the boundaries of a *githaka* are fixed according to the original claims by the *mbari* founder(s). There will therefore arise the need for acquiring extra land, or rights in extra land, outside the *githaka* for the use of members of an expanding *mbari*. This will happen in one of two ways: either a segment of the *mbari* will split off and move to new unclaimed land elsewhere, or members will acquire rights outside the *githaka* while still remaining members of the *mbari*.

Not all *mbari* however were able to sell their land: in some cases the founder(s) or a descendant of the founder(s) have left a *kirumi* (a testamentary decision) forbidding the sale on penalty of supernatural punishment.

All land-rights acquired from another *mbari* other than sale must be seen in the light of four basic principles:

(a) The distinction between the land itself and the cultivated soil (*mugunda*); right are given to the latter only[292]: the rights are of use of the land.
(b) Land is a loan[293]—right of redemption is never lost by the males of the *mbari* (even wives have no more than user rights; although they are the media of inheritance, they do not own the land).
(c) The enjoyment of a tenancy is dependent on use: usually a landowner cannot evict a tenant who is using the loaned land,[294] unless he needs it himself.
(d) "The relationship of the Kikuyu and his tenant rests essentially on a basis of friendship, which is more than a mere pretence."[295]

There are three types of contractual tenant-relationship:

(i) *Muguri:* A *muguri* is a person who receives the use of land against a loan of livestock, on the condition that redemption can take place at any time. The transaction is initiated by the land-owner, who announces that he wishes to borrow stock. A *muguri* cannot lend the land to others. *Muguri*-rights may be inherited. The word *muguri* has come to mean an outright purchaser of land, who then has full and permanent rights over it. But the seller is still supposed to initiate the transaction.[296]

(ii) *Muhoi:* A *muhoi* is one who acquires cultivation rights without payment, on a basis of friendship; the relationship may be inherited, but a *muhoi* may plant only temporary crops, may not take on other *ahoi*, and must leave when asked to do so; a *muhoi* may terminate the relationship by ceasing cultivation. No rent is paid, although annual tribute of beer and first fruits is given to the owner; if rent were paid, the relationship would change its character.[297]

[290] K.L.C. Evidence 1932, I, pp. 991, 1004; Maxwell Report, 1929, p. 18; Kenyatta, 1938, pp. 29, 177; Tate, 1911, p. 297.

[291] Kenyatta, 1938, p. 33.

[292] C. Dundas, 1915, p. 298.

[293] Barlow, 1932, p. 64.

[294] Beech, 1917, p. 137; Maxwell Report, 1929, p. 26.

[295] Maxwell Report, p. 13.

[296] Maxwell Report, 1929, pp. 15–27, Appendix, p. 53; Barlow, 1932, p. 66; Kenyatta, 1938, pp. 38–9; Lambert, 1950, pp. 96 ff.

[297] Maxwell Report, 1929, pp. 15–34, Appendix, pp. 10, 44, 54, 56; Barlow, 1932, p. 65; Kenyatta, 1938, p. 35; Beech, 1917, pp. 56–7; C. Dundas, 1915, p. 298.

(iii) *Muthami:* A *muthami* is one who acquires building rights on another *mbari*'s *githaka*. Most *athami* are *ahoi* or *aguri* who have also acquired these rights, although the relationships are quite distinct.[298]

The second category of tenant-relationships consists of those based on status-ties. These rights are part of the complex of rights and duties forming the relationships of *muthoni*, *mwendia ruhiu*, *muciarua* and *ndungata*.

(i) The right deriving from the *muthoni* (affinal) tie is usually that given to a son-in-law by his father-in-law; this right cannot be refused if the son-in-law is in need of land. It is not, of course, heritable. Other affinal ties, such as that between brothers-in-law, also give such rights. The affines of a *muhoi* or *muguri* have no such rights in the land on which they are tenants: the lending party must be a member of the *mbari* owning the land.[299]

(ii) The status of *mwendia ruhiu* ("the man who sells his sword") is essentially that of the *genitor* of children who belong to the mother's *mbari* or the *mbari* of a widow's husband: he is a begetter of children who are not affiliated to him. The land rights which are part of his status are used by the woman with whom he is living, and are not heritable from him, since the children inherit from their mother's family.[300] He also has ritual functions: Lambert calls him a "professional taint-remover", without explaining the expression.[301]

(iii) A *muciarua* is a man (often a foreigner) who has no rights in any *githaka* and is "adopted" by a wealthy man, given a wife and land; his children belong to the adopted *mbari* and inherit from it.[302]

(iv) A *ndungata* is a person who attaches himself to a rich man and is given a wife and land.[303] It may be another term for *muciarua*.

It should be noted that the common focus of all these status-relationships is a woman; this is the most obvious in the case of a *muthoni*, but it is true of the other relationships also.

The only person who can take on tenants of these various kinds is a *mwene githaka* (owner of a *githaka*). The term applies to the original owner of a *githaka* (before it becomes *mbari* land) and to the head of any component family of the *mbari* which is allotted a portion of the *githaka*. The *muramati* would be referred to as *mwene githaka* of his own portion of the *githaka*.[304]

The council of elders has two main roles with regard to land. In it is vested the control of public land ("communal" land as it is often called) and utilities, and it also acts when there is need for arbitration between *mbari* over land matters. The basic principle involved is stated by the K.L.C. Evidence: "Under the *githaka* system no land is common, but certain rights are common, and the right to depasture cattle on any land not cultivated or specially reserved in accordance with custom is one of these."[305] The first of these common rights is that of grazing, which is the chief use of fallow and uncultivated land. Grazing rights are irrespective of *githaka* boundaries, and any person may graze livestock on unclaimed land. There are also permanent public grazing grounds, on which no individual claims can be made at all.[306]

An *mbari* has the right to close fallow land to other people's livestock by putting

[298] Maxwell Report, 1929, pp. 15–34, Appendix, p. 55; Kenyatta, 1938, p. 34; Barlow, 1932, p. 66.

[299] Maxwell Report, 1929, pp. 24–6, 34, 53–6, Appendix, p. 56; C. Dundas, 1915, p. 298; Beech, 1917, p. 55; Barlow, 1932, p. 65; Hobley, 2, 1910, p. 137; Lambert, 1950, p. 136.

[300] Maxwell Report, 1929, pp. 26, 34, 72, Appendix, p. 57; C. Dundas, 1915, p. 295; Hobley, 1938, p. 156; Lambert, 1950, pp. 105 ff.

[301] Lambert, 1956, p. 54.

[302] Kenyatta, 1938, p. 22; Maxwell Report, 1929, pp. 24, 26, 34.

[303] Humphrey, 1924, p. 23; Cagnolo, 1933, p. 212.

[304] Beech, 1917, pp. 56, 137; C. Dundas, 1915, p. 298; Kenyatta, 1938, pp. 21, 32.

[305] K.L.C. Evidence, 1932, I, p. 992.

[306] Maxwell Report, 1929, Appendix, p. 44; K.L.C. Report, 1932, paras, 139, 204; Beech, 1917, pp. 47, 52; Cagnolo, 1933, p. 34; Kenyatta, 1938, p. 36.

up certain marks; if it does so it is in order to rest the land only, and it must not graze its own cattle on that area.[307]

Similarly, rights to timber and grass on the land of an *mbari* are common to all, as are rights to salt-licks and mineral springs, public meeting- and dancing-places, public roads and paths, water and sacred groves. Most of these are on *mbari* land, but rights to them may be exercised by any members of the community.[308]

As in other matters the district elders have powers in land matters. They arbitrate in inter-*mbari* land disputes, as in other cases. They may exchange land with a public utility found on it for another piece, and act as witnesses in the ceremony of marking the boundary at the sale of land and at other (unspecified) land transactions.[309] According to the Maxwell Report, the council of elders can also intervene in the internal affairs of an *mbari* and act as final sanction behind the decisions of the *muramati*. A member of the *mbari* or a tenant who demurs at an order of the *muramati* may be arraigned before the council of elders.[310] Today the *kiama* handles a large number of land cases, dealing with such matters as inheritance, compensation and tenancies.[311]

Land Tenure Among the Northern Tribes

The Maxwell Report states that the "*githaka* system" is not found in Embu and Meru.[312]

In Embu "there are large distinct areas of land belonging to each division mostly alternating in ridges as the land was taken with the increase of population. It was taken up in village groups (*itura*) Any man from an *itura* of one division wishing to cultivate on the land of another *itura* of the same division would have to consult the elders of that locality. . . . He would take up ordinary status in the new *itura* according to his age and cannot be evicted. There is frequent movement of this kind."[313] Beech states that families on a ridge are of the same clan.[314] Boundaries are marked between areas of land belonging to different clans in Meru, but not in Chuka except where they adjoin those of the other division. In Meru there are no *aramati*, control of a *githaka* being by a group of elders composed of those elders of the clan who are members of the *mbari* concerned and live on its *githaka*. Within the *githaka* the permission of the elders of the clan is required for clearing new land.[315] In Embu the land units are *githaka* held by *mbari*. The right to cultivate virgin land on a *githaka* is not confined to that *mbari* but extends to any members of the clan concerned, provided permission is asked of the *mbari* elders.[316]

Among these tribes it seems, therefore, although the material is very sketchy, that the land-holding unit is the *mbari* or joint family, but the land of an *mbari* usually forms part of a block of land held by a clan; unlike the situation in Kikuyu, the clan may be a local unit. It is clear from the fact that cultivation rights in a *githaka* are common to all the members of a clan that the *mbari* is by no means the independent group that it is in Kikuyu; it is regarded as merely a component segment of the clan, although it may manage its own internal affairs. Control is by the clan council, although it may be delegated to those of its members who are members of the *mbari* concerned.

[307] Cagnolo, 1933, p. 34; Maxwell Report, 1929, Appendix, pp. 11, 20, 44, 59; Kenyatta, 1938, p. 36.

[308] Beech, 1917, p. 54; C. Dundas, 1921, p. 272; Kenyatta, 1938, p. 36; K.L.C. Evidence, 1932, I, pp. 500–1; Maxwell Report, 1929, Appendix, pp. 14, 26, 32; Hobley, 1938, p. 96.

[309] Kenyatta, 1938, pp. 31, 36, 38.

[310] Maxwell Report, 1929, Appendix, pp. 36, 42.

[311] Phillips, 1945, pp. 48, 59.

[312] Maxwell Report, 1929, p. 35.

[313] Maxwell Report, 1929, Appendix, p. 15.

[314] Beech, 1917, p. 52.

[315] Maxwell Report, 1929, Appendix, pp. 19, 24, 29.

[316] Maxwell Report, 1929, p. 19.

Certain other rights are common to the clan. Chief of these are grazing, hunting, use of timber, salt-licks, soda, ochre, etc.; these were controlled by the *njuri* members of the clan concerned.[317]

Tenant relationships are similar to those found in Kikuyu: *muguri, muhoi, muthami, muthoni* and *muciarua* are mentioned.[318] The difference is that the tenant is in relationship with the clan, through its elders, rather than with the *mbari* through its representative, the *muramati*.

Slavery

According to Routledge, the Kikuyu had no slavery in any form, and did not make raids to capture slaves.[319] Von Höhnel writes of Masai and Kamba girl-slaves and states that deserters from caravans would be made slaves when caught by the Kikuyu; he adds that the Kikuyu has the right of life and death over his slaves, but must pay compensation for injury done to the slaves of another.[320] It is possible that von Höhnel's account is incorrect, since he was only in the country for a very short time.

MAIN CULTURAL FEATURES

Physical and Mental Characteristics

Tables showing heights and weights of Kikuyu males and females are given by Orr and Gilks,[321] and similar tables for Chuka, Embu and Mwimbi by Orde-Browne.[322] Opinions vary as to the general physical characteristics of the Kikuyu: some writers state that the Kikuyu are strong and muscular,[323] others that they are slender and slightly built;[324] all describe them as being of medium height only.

Dress

Today, a form of European dress is usually worn by men, and often by women. The following description refers to the indigenous dress only.

Men

The traditional dress and ornaments of a Kikuyu varied according to his age. The usual clothing of men was made of goat-skins, although when working in the fields only a banana leaf was worn round the loins. At dances an apron was sufficient. Hats and caps were not generally worn, although a head-covering copied from the Masai, made from an ox-stomach, might be seen.[325]

Ornaments of metal were worn on the neck, arms and legs. The Tharaka wore leather leggings. Ear ornaments consisted of various wire and iron rings and discs attached to the cartilage and a cylinder of wood in the lobe. The lobes were pierced before circumcision.[326]

The Kikuyu proper did not file their teeth, nor pierce the nose or lips. The Embu, Chuka and Mbere chipped the two upper incisors.[327] Men sometimes had three or four

[317] Laughton, 1944, p. 5; K.L.C. Evidence, 1932, I, p. 388; Maxwell Report, 1929, Appendix, p. 32; Orde-Brown, 1925, p. 68.

[318] Maxwell Report, 1929, p. 22, Appendix, pp. 29, 32; Beech, 1917, p. 139; Phillips, 1945, p. 98.

[319] Routledge, 1910, p. 16.

[320] Von Höhnel, 1894, I, pp. 315, 359.

[321] Orr and Gilks, 1931, pp. 77 ff.; see also Danby, 1953.

[322] Orde-Browne, 1916, pp. 232–3.

[323] Routledge, 1910, p. 19; von Höhnel, 1894, I, p. 354; Hinde, 1901, p. 17; Crawshay, 1902, pp. 27–9; Jackson, 1930, p. 171.

[324] Cagnolo, 1933, p. 19; Tate, 1904, p. 132.

[325] Routledge, 1910, pp. 26, 30, 34–5 (illus.); Cagnolo, 1933, pp. 32, 40, 205; Kenyatta, 1938, p. 92; Tate, 1, 1904, p. 133; von Höhnel, I, p. 355; Champion, 1912, p. 74; Orde-Brown, 1925, pp. 134–7.

[326] Routledge, 1910, pp. 31–5 (illus.); Tate, 1, 1904, p. 134; von Höhnel, 1894, I, p. 355; Crawshay, 1902, p. 30; Champion, 1912, pp. 75–6; Braunholtz, 1921; Boyers, 1911, p. 300; Stigand, 1913, p. 247.

[327] Routledge, 1910, p. 33; Orde-Browne, 1916, p. 228; 1925, p. 139.

raised scars on the loins. Adolescents sometimes adorned their faces with red and blue paint.[328]

Men had many ways of hairdressing; Routledge states that "every little district has, in the case of men, its own styles of adorning the hair". A man frequently had his head shaved, on various ritual and ceremonial occasions, but at other times there were several styles for the hair—string, feathers or mud being added to the hair to lengthen or colour it. Among the Northern tribes men with a circumcised child shaved their heads. All other body hair was removed with tweezers.[329]

Men's war-dress was copied from that of the Masai; the hair was dressed into a pigtail, war-marks and special ornaments were worn and a Masai-type shield and spear were carried.[330]

Male children were naked, but female children wore at least a leather apron.[331]

Women

Kikuyu women wore a leather apron, a "petticoat" and a skin cloak. Among the Northern tribes they wore a skin under-apron and a "petticoat"; the Mwimbi wore no under-apron. They wore no hats or footgear.[332]

From initiation to marriage women wore a brow-band of beads and discs; a necklace was the first betrothal present; an iron collaret was a marriage present from her father-in-law, and copper ear-rings, the sign of a woman with an uninitiated child. A bead girdle was worn by all women. Armlets, anklets and most ear ornaments were similar to those worn by men, but Embu women wore only a small ear-ring.[333]

A woman shaved her head entirely except for a small tuft at the back of the head, and this was removed when old. Hair was left to grow if she was sick.[334]

Women sometimes adorned the abdomen with small raised scars. Among the Northern tribes, especially the Mwimbi, women cicatrized their necks and bodies.[335]

Life Cycle

BIRTH

We here describe the traditional customs, many of which are today no longer observed.

Before confinement the woman observes certain food taboos.[336] During the confinement, all weapons and iron articles must be removed from the hut, and the husband must sleep in the *thingira*.[337]

As soon as the child is born, the mother emits five screams if it is a boy and four if it is a girl; the father then cuts five or four sugar-canes which are eaten by the mother and the child; the scraps of cane are placed at the right of the hut entrance if a boy, at the left if a girl. The child is washed and oiled. The placenta is disposed of by being covered with grain and grass on uncultivated land. The husband sacrifices a goat if the birth is difficult, and, if the after-birth is difficult, a medicine man is called to whip the hut.[338]

[328] Routledge, 1910, p. 33; Tate, 2, 1904, p. 255.
[329] Routledge, 1910, pp. 26–30 (illus.); Tate, I, 1904, p. 134; von Höhnel, 1894, 1, pp. 354–5; Crawshay, 1902, p. 29; Orde-Browne, 1925, pp. 92, 137–8; Champion, 1912, p. 77.
[330] Routledge, 1910, p. 15 (illus.); Cagnolo, 1933, pp. 99–100; Hobley, 1910, p. 132; Orde-Browne, 1925, p. 134; Gurney, 1929, p. 204; Eliot, 1905, p. 127; Jackson, 1930, p. 171.
[331] Routledge, 1910, p. 139.
[332] Routledge, 1910, pp. 139–41 (illus.); Kenyatta, 1938, p. 92; Tate, 1, 1903, p. 133; von Höhnel, 1894, 1, p. 355; Crawshay, 1902, p. 31; Orde-Browne, 1925, pp. 134–5; Gurney, 1929, p. 205; Champion, 1912, p. 75.
[333] Routledge, 1910, p. 140 (illus.); Tate, 1, 1904, pp. 134–5; Arkell-Hardwick, 1903, p. 316; Champion, 1912, pp. 76–7; Orde-Browne, 1925, p. 88.
[334] Routledge, 1910, p. 140; Tate, 1, 1904, p. 133; Champion, 1912, p. 77; Orde-Browne, 1925, p. 92.
[335] Routledge, 1910, p. 141; Orde-Browne, 1916, p. 228; 1925, p. 139.
[336] Routledge, 1910, p. 147.
[337] Hobley, 1938, p. 160; Champion, 1912, p. 83.
[338] Cagnolo, 1933, p. 64; Orde-Browne, 1925, p. 80; Routledge, 1910, p. 147.

The mother is in seclusion in her hut for five days after the birth of a boy and four after that of a girl. Only the "immediate woman friends and attendants" may enter. At the end of this period the mother is shaved, the father sacrifices a sheep and normal life is resumed. Childbirth does not cause ritual uncleanness (*thahu*) and so no purification by a magician is necessary. The mother pays a ceremonial visit to her fields to gather arum lily roots and sweet potatoes (in the Northern tribes she gathers yams). During the seclusion period, no member of the family may wash in the river, nor may the hut be swept or fire taken from it to kindle elsewhere.[339] At some time after birth a small boy and girl are sent to the river to fetch water.[340]

The child is named at birth. The first child is given the name of the paternal grandparent, and the second that of the maternal grandparent, according to sex; this applies to the children of each wife. Kenyatta states: "The first male is regarded as perpetuating the existence of the man's father, the second as perpetuating that of the woman's father. The first and second female children fulfil the same ritual duty to the souls of their grandmothers on both sides."[341] Among the Northern tribes, if a child dies, the next-born child may be named after an animal rather than a grandparent; "certain sections regard the child as having some occult connection with its name animal, and, in consequence, both the child and its father are forbidden to harm the animal in any way." A second name, that of the man who supports him during the circumcision ceremony, is given to a boy at initiation.[342] There are no other references to what may be a system of personal totems.

Twins are said to have been unlucky, and, if first-born, in the past to have been killed (or sometimes only the second was killed); but twins are more usually given away to foster-parents. Unless this is done, the women will not bear children again. Later born twins are not killed. Triplets are always killed, as is a child born feet first, and a child cutting its upper teeth first may be killed. The killing is by suffocation, but it is not stated by whom. A child whose mother was pregnant before menstruation is killed, as is one whose mother dies before it cuts its teeth. If a child touches the ground at birth a goat must be sacrificed. A man has the right to kill an adulterine child borne by his wife. A woman who bears twins or a child who cuts its upper teeth first must cohabit with a *mwendia ruhiu* (the relationship, if any, is unspecified); when she has borne a child to him she may cohabit again with her husband.[343]

Between birth and initiation the child goes through various ceremonies which clearly mark the stages in his acceptance as a full member of the tribe. Routledge states that when the child is "very small" the father puts wristlets of goat-skin on him; he then "becomes a MKikuyu"; there are further rites, the relations eat together, and the husband and wife resume normal sex relations.[344] There is a similar ceremony among the Tharaka when the child is about six months old.[345] Among the Meru sexual relations between husband and wife are not resumed until the child is weaned, about the second year,[346] and there is also a rite to mark the cutting of the first teeth.[347] Cagnolo states that weaning takes place at six or seven years,[348] but this would seem to be wrong. Routledge mentions a rite which marks the beginning of the child's economic activities, minding the goats, which occurs when about five

[339] Routledge, 1910, p. 147; Cagnolo, 1933, p. 65; Champion, 1912, p. 83; Orde-Browne, 1925, p p. 80–1; Holding, 1942, p. 60.

[340] Routledge, 1910, p. 50.

[341] Routledge, 1910, p. 149; Kenyatta, 1938, pp. 15, 164; Tate, 2, 1904, p. 264; but see Cagnolo, 1933, p. 63; Hobley, 1938, p. 260.

[342] Orde-Browne, 1925, pp. 78–80; Laughton, 1944, p. 9.

[343] Routledge, 1910, pp. 194–50; Cagnolo, 1933, pp. 62–3; Hobley, 1938, pp. 154–6; C. Dundas, 1915, p. 301; 1921, pp. 233–4; Orde-Browne, 1925, p. 78.

[344] Routledge, 1910, p. 150.

[345] Champion, 1912, p. 84.

[346] Laughton, 1944, p. 10; Holding, 1942, p. 60.

[347] Orde-Browne, 1925, pp. 81–2.

[348] Cagnolo, 1933, p. 67.

years old.[349] When a boy "reaches a certain age" the mother removes one of his lower incisors (Crawshay says two incisors are removed).[350]

SECOND BIRTH

The most important of the *rites de passage* between birth and initiation is that of "second birth", *guciaruo ringi*, *guciaruo gwa keri* or *guciariruo mburi* (to be born of a goat). This rite is undergone by both sexes of all clans. Until a child has undergone the rite he cannot assist in the disposal of his father's body after death, be initiated, inherit property, or take part in ritual, depending on the "guild". The essential part of the rite is a re-enactment of the birth (if the mother is dead a proxy is appointed who is afterwards regarded by the child "as his own mother"); the child is placed between the mother's legs, and bound to her by a goat intestine. This is cut and the child imitates the crying of a newborn child. The mother is then shaved, the hut swept out, and a formal visit is made to the fields to collect arum lily roots.[351]

INITIATION

The initiation ceremonies of all the Kikuyu tribes include a physical operation for both sexes: the boys undergo circumcision, the girls clitoridectomy. The word for the physical operation, *irua*, is used for the whole rite.[352] Among the Kikuyu proper boys are usually initiated between the ages of 15 and 18 years, and girls between 10 and 15. A novice must not have had sexual intercourse.[353] Among the Mwimbi the age of boys at initiation is from 12 to 16, and girls are a little older; in Chuka the age is a little more, while in Embu it is much younger, boys often being only 11 or so years old. The operation among the Tharaka is "prepubescent".[354]

Initiations take place yearly, unless crops have failed or there are other signs of divine displeasure. They are held at the beginning of the wet season, when the crops have been sown and before they are gathered: at this time little labour is needed in the fields. The ceremony cannot begin at full moon, since this would be unlucky.[355] Tate says that boys and girls are initiated at different months and during different rains, i.e. in April–May or November, but K. R. Dundas states that both sexes undergo the ceremony in the same months, but that the season depends on whether they live in east or west Kikuyu.[356]

Only girls are initiated in those years when the *thongoya* plant blooms (every ten years)[357]; this may apply to Nyeri only.

The available descriptions of Kikuyu initiation rites are confusing and very different. The chief reason for this, apart from the fact that most of the descriptions are apparently based on the observation of only one, or even only part of one, ceremony, is that the Kikuyu have two forms of rite, according to whether the novice is a member of the Kikuyu or Masai guild. The physical operation is the same in both cases, but the remainder of the rites is quite different.[358] In addition, each clan practises a different series of rites.[359] However, certain rites appear to be common to all the different guild and clan ceremonies. The most satisfactory procedure is to describe these common rites, without attempting to describe the many variations.[360]

[349] Routledge, 1910, p. 150.

[350] Cagnolo, 1933, p. 77; Cayzac, 1910, p. 312; Crawshay, 1902, p. 31.

[351] There is a good account in Routledge, 1910, pp. 152–3; also Hobley, 1938, pp. 77–8; Cagnolo, 1933, p. 84; Orde-Browne, 1925, pp. 82–3.

[352] Kenyatta, 1938, p. 134; Leakey, 1931, p. 277; see below, p. 58.

[353] Routledge, 1910, p. 155; Cagnolo, 1933, p. 85; Kenyatta, op. cit., pp. 107, 136, 162; Bugeau, 1911, p. 616.

[354] Orde-Browne, 1913, p. 137; 1915, pp. 65, 68; Lambert, 1947, p. 3.

[355] Routledge, 1910, pp. 156–7; Cagnolo, 1933, p. 86; Hobley, 1938, p. 83; Tate, 1911, p. 285; Orde-Browne, 1913, p. 137; 1915, p. 65.

[356] Tate, 1911, p. 285 K. R. Dundas, 1909, p. 38.

[357] Cagnolo, 1933, p. 198.

[358] Hobley, 1938, pp. 77–89; Cagnolo, 1933, p. 83.

[359] Kenyatta, 1938, pp. 138, 151.

[360] The fullest descriptions are those of Routledge, 1910, pp. 154 ff.; Kenyatta, 1938, pp. 130 ff.; Hobley, 1938, pp. 77 ff.; Cagnolo, op. cit., pp. 81 ff. (all for the Kikuyu); and Orde-Browne, 1913 (Mwimbi); Orde-Browne, 1915 (Chuka).

The universal and, it may be considered, the essential rites which make up the Kikuyu initiation ceremony are:

(*a*) Preliminary ceremonies, culminating in the Great Dance.
(*b*) Circumcision.
(*c*) The novices' retirement.
(*d*) Aggregation rites.

(*a*) ***Preliminary Ceremonies***

The various descriptions are not in agreement about the preliminary ceremonies, and there are clearly many omissions in the material, due probably to the fact that these ceremonies may take place some time before the actual day of circumcision, and may not have been observed by the various writers.

Near the time of initiation, the child's ears are pierced. Four goats are given back to the husband from the bridewealth transferred for the child's mother, and the mother's brother is given five goats for his "permission" for the piercing.[361]

Three or four months before the circumcision date the novices begin to go about the countryside in bands, singing and dancing.[362]

Kenyatta states that three or four days before the circumcision the novices go to the homestead where they are to be circumcised, and are "adopted" by the elder and his wife. Their sponsor, according to Bugeau, "will acquire certain rights over his adopted children, all the rights belonging to the bonds of affinity". Information as to who this elder is and the relationship between him and the novices he "adopts" is not given. The night is spent singing and dancing in a ceremony "which is supposed to keep the gods awake. This ceremony is considered an act of communion with the ancestral god (*murungu*), whose protection is invoked to guide and protect the initiates."[363] Routledge states that on the day before the Great Dance the novices drink a potion to ward off evil spirits.[364] It is clear that the novices are ritually prepared for the coming period by being put in a close relationship with God.

In the descriptions of the ceremonies which culminate in the Great Dance, the shaving and anointing of the novices appear to be invariable rites, although they take different forms and occur at different points in the proceedings. It would seem that the social function of these rites is to continue the process of separating the novices from society and placing them in a close relationship with God. Shaving and anointing occur before the Great Dance (Kenyatta and Hobley), after the dance but on the same day (Routledge), and after the circumcision (Cagnolo). The rite of anointing is called *kurathima ciana*—to bless the children. Boys are marked on the face with white earth called *ira*[365] by the elder "who holds the senior office in the ceremonial council" (Kenyatta). The ceremony takes place in the circumcision homestead, and the children pass in front of the elder "according to their order of adoption". Girls are anointed with oil by an old woman, on the head, neck and feet. According to Hobley, this rite occurs for the children of the Masai guild only, and is accompanied by the shaving of the novices' heads. Routledge adds that the elders who perform the rite are regarded as the "father" and "mother" of the novices: they are presumably their sponsors, although this is not explicitly stated.[366]

The Great Dance[367] is clearly regarded as the most important part of the ritual

[361] Cagnolo, 1933, pp. 77–8; Kenyatta, 1938, p. 107; Holding, 1942, p. 60; Routledge, 1910, p. 157.

[362] Routledge, 1910, pp. 155–6 (illus.).

[363] Kenyatta, 1938, pp. 136–7; Cagnolo, 1933, p. 84; Bugeau, 1911, p. 619.

[364] Routledge, 1910, p. 157.

[365] *Ira* is a white diatomaceous earth, thought to be the snow on Mount Kenya, the home of God. Hobley, 1938, p. 83; Kenyatta, 1938, p. 137; Routledge, 1910, p. 253; Cagnolo, 1933, p. 188.

[366] Kenyatta, 1938, p. 137; Hobley, 1938, pp. 83–4; Routledge, 1910, p. 160; Cagnolo, 1933, p. 90.

[367] *Matuumo* (Kenyatta, 1938, p. 138) or *Mambura* (Routledge, 1910, p. 158; Hobley, 1938, p. 80). Cagnolo, 1933, pp. 84, 91, 92, 93, 113, uses *mambura* to refer to any ritual act, especially ritual intercourse.

leading up to actual circumcision. The ceremony begins with several hours' dancing at or near the circumcision homestead. At the dancing ground an arch of sugar-canes and banana-tree stems is erected, so that evil spirits cannot enter: this is the custom of the Masai guild, the Kikuyu guild using other plants. After the dance the novices leave the homestead and go to a nearby sacred tree; the girls walk first, and the boys race. The winner of the race is made the leader of the age-set. When they reach the tree the boys beat the trunk with staves, throw staves over the tree, and some of them climb the tree and break off boughs and bark which they throw to the waiting girls and "feminine relations", who collect them. The leaves are later used by the novices' sponsors during the circumcision and also for the novices' beds.[368]

The novices then take the "tribal oath" (Kenyatta). They return to the circumcision homestead, not looking back on the way. As they enter under the ceremonial arch they are sprayed with honey, milk and medicines by their sponsor; this is the "ceremony of parting", *gutiihira ciana* (to spray the children with honey).[369]

Routledge mentions another rite at this point. A boy climbs on to the homestead roof and discovers hidden objects there which "either refer to the evolution of the boy into the young man" or are presents from friends and relatives. The staves and head-dresses which they have been wearing are piled on the roof and the boy jumps down, catches and beats a child from among the onlookers: reports say that formerly this child was killed.[370]

(b) Circumcision[371]

After the Great Dance the boys dance all night, while the girls rest in the house of the "mother". In the morning the boys divide into two or more parties for the circumcision itself: the composition of these groups is not stated. The boys bathe in the river, while their mothers and other relatives watch. While bathing they drop the leaves collected during the Great Dance into the water "as a sign of drowning their childhood behaviour and forgetting about it for ever". Their heads are shaven. They return singing mournful songs, in which their parents join. They then go to the *iteri*, the site of the operation. The girls also bathe and go to the *iteri*; no men are allowed near; water in which an axehead has rested all night is thrown on the sexual organs.[372]

The boys sit in a row on clean hides. They are supported by their sponsors, holding the leaves which were taken from the sacred tree. As soon as the operator has performed the operation the sponsor covers the boy with a cloak. The girls are operated on similarly, supported by two sponsors. The novices must not flinch or cry out. The girls are also covered with cloaks after the operation.[373]

Among the Northern tribes the rite is similar in essentials, but with different details. The actual operation is in two parts, with further rites between them.[374]

[368] Kenyatta, 1938, pp. 139–40; Routledge, 1910, pp. 158–9; Cagnolo, 1933, pp. 87–8; Hobley, 1938, pp. 80–4; Barlow, 1915, pp. 42–4.

[369] Kenyatta, 1938, pp. 141–2; Routledge, 1910, p. 160; Hobley, 1938, p. 85.

[370] Routledge, 1910, p. 161.

[371] The operation performed on boys differs slightly from one tribe to another; the Kikuyu cut off the prepuce entirely, the Meru and Mwimbi pierce it by a slit through which the *glans penis* is put, while the Chuka, Embu and Mbere remove the entire prepuce but in a different manner from the Kikuyu. Among the Kikuyu the girls undergo clitoridectomy and, according to Routledge, the *labia minora* are also removed; among the Embu and Meru tribes the *labia minora* and part of the *labia majora* are removed. See Kenyatta, 1938, p. 146; Routledge, 1910, p. 164; Tate, 1, 1904, p. 265; Orde-Browne, 1913, pp. 138–40 and 1915, pp. 65–8.

[372] Kenyatta, 1938, pp. 145–6; Routledge, 1910, p. 163; Hobley, 1938, p. 85; Cagnolo, 1933, p. 88.

[373] Routledge, 1910, pp. 163–4; Kenyatta, 1938, pp. 145–6; Cagnolo, 1933, p. 89; Bugeau, 1911, pp. 619–22.

[374] Concise accounts are given by Orde-Browne, 1913 and 1915; also 1925, pp. 84 ff.

(*c*) *The Novices' Retirement*

After the operation, the boys retire to temporary huts, *kiganda*, where they are to spend the period of seclusion; they are cared for by young men. On the ninth day members of the Kikuyu guild return home; members of the Masai guild leave on the fourth day and spend until the next new moon shooting birds. Among the Northern tribes the seclusion period is longer, and for the first few days the novices are fed on milk only. The girls live in one of their mothers' huts and are fed by others in a ceremonial manner.[375]

(*d*) *Aggregation Rites*

It is difficult to make a coherent account of these rites, owing to the different opinions as to the length of time they take. A few days after the operation boys of the Kikuyu guild have certain plants put in their ears, which are later changed for wooden cylinders; boys of the Masai guild wear copper ear-rings. This is a sign that they have changed status and become men. Their heads are shaven. Later the *kiganda* is burnt and they return home, where they are anointed by their parents, who have ritual intercourse. Kenyatta states that for three or four months they do not work but go round the countryside singing and dancing. At the end of this period they return to the circumcision homestead, their heads are shaved and they discard the initiation dress and ornaments. They are then given warriors' equipment.[376] Lambert states that for this Kikuyu guild this is done after they have taken part in a "ceremonial rape" of a woman who is a stranger to them.[377]

Kenyatta states that the rite of second birth takes place after initiation: this would seem to be incorrect since no child can be initiated without having undergone the rite. He adds that the new members of society adopt new kinship terms between themselves and the "father" and "mother" of the initiation.[378]

BETROTHAL AND MARRIAGE

Girls do not marry before sixteen or seventeen years of age. According to Kenyatta, the choice of spouse is made by the persons themselves, but Dundas states that infant betrothal is common, bridewealth often being transferred then.[379]

The boy's proposal is conveyed to the girl by his age-mates. Bridewealth (*ruraacio*)[380] is then collected by the boy from his father and taken by him to the girl's mother. It is transferred in instalments over a period, and may even be deferred during the girl's life, the girl's father then having claims on the bridewealth received for his granddaughters; Dundas states that this occurs in perhaps one in every five marriages.[381] The betrothal is celebrated by the ceremony of "pouring out the blood of unity" between the *mbari* concerned. The marriage date is then decided, and the girl publicly signifies her consent at a ceremony at which presents are exchanged between the families and special dances performed.[382]

The bride is captured in mock fight. Kenyatta and Cagnolo state that she is taken by the man's "female relatives", including his mother, while Routledge states that she is taken by the boy's age-mates. She is defended by her female relatives. She is visited in the evening by her age-mates of both sexes who sing a mourning song which signifies the break between the bride and her age-set. She is kept in seclusion in her

[375] Routledge, 1910, p. 164; Kenyatta, 1938, pp. 147–8; Bugeau, 1911, pp. 622–3; Hobley, 1938, p. 80; Orde-Browne, 1913, p. 138.

[376] Routledge, 1910, pp. 165–6; Kenyatta, 1938, pp. 151–3; Hobley, 1938, p. 86; Cagnolo, 1933, pp. 90–4; Tate, 2, 1904, p. 265; Bugeau, 1911, p. 624–5.

[377] Lambert, 1956, p. 53–4.

[378] Kenyatta, 1938, pp. 149–51.

[379] Kenyatta, 1938, p. 163; C. Dundas, 1915, p. 284; Routledge, 1910, pp. 124–5.

[380] Bridewealth consists of cattle, sheep and goats; among the Kikuyu the amount is that given for the girl's mother; among the Tharaka it never varies in amount. (C. Dundas, 1915, pp. 285–6; 1921, p. 253; Kenyatta, 1938, p. 168; Routledge, 1910, p. 125; Cagnolo, 1933, p. 108).

[381] C. Dundas, 1915, pp. 285–6; 1921, pp. 254–5 Routledge, 1910, pp. 125–8; Kenyatta, 1938, p. 168; Cagnolo, 1933, p. 109; Tate, 1910, p. 246; Orde-Browne, 1925, p. 75; Gurney, 1929, p. 206.

[382] Kenyatta, 1938, pp. 165–70; Routledge, 1910, pp. 126–8; Cagnolo, 1933, pp. 109–10.

hut for several days. At the end of this period she visits her parents, led as though blind by a girl of her husband's family. The marriage is said by Routledge to be consummated at the end of the period of seclusion, but Cagnolo states that it occurs on the night she is brought from her parents' home.[383]

The bride's father-in-law "warms" her hut by allotting her livestock and land, and by giving her arum lily roots and an iron collaret. Her own mother provides her with new hearth-stones from the river bed and with cooking pots.[384]

Among the Tharaka all those men who have had sexual relations with her before her marriage bring her a goat.[385]

There are certain sexual taboos on a married woman: she may not have sexual intercourse outside her hut, while her husband is away, while food is being cooked, or before the children are in bed.[386]

Death and Burial

The Kikuyu and Masai guilds[387] have different methods of burial.

Only persons who have reached a high grade of elderhood are buried with a certain amount of ceremonial. The grave is dug in the bush near the dead man's village by the man's first-born sons by different wives: they must be initiated. The corpse of a man is buried on its right side, doubled up and with hand under head, that of a woman on its left side. It is placed either in or on an oxhide, according to guild. The man's intimate personal possessions are buried with him, the others put on the grave with the material from his dismantled hut on top of all; the site is then left.[388]

The bodies of other persons were placed in the bush, or the body might be left in the hut, a hole being made for the hyenas to enter. A person who is sick and likely to die might be exposed in the bush before death.[388a]

At a man's death, a "poor clansman" of the dead man is brought and has ritual intercourse with the senior widow; "he generally lives on in the village and is looked upon as a step-father to the children". The sons who have buried a father, and also the entire village, must be purified: until this is done the members of the village must observe sexual continence. Hobley describes the purification rites, during which the villagers wear their skin garments turned inside out and smeared with latex from the sacred tree. It is not stated who performs the purification ceremony, but presumably it is a *mundu mugo* (medicine man). When dead, a person may not be spoken of nor his name mentioned.[389]

Traditional Religious Beliefs and Ritual

The Kikuyu sacrifice both to the spirits of the ancestors and to God. "The belief in the ancestral spirits. . . is the predominating spiritual factor in the minds of the great majority of the people", but, as Kenyatta points out, the two sets of beliefs and the practices associated with them cannot be separated. "Gikuyu religion has definitely two departments. Both are really vital; they function in unison, but in different spheres. . . . For example . . . when a sacrifice is made to the High God on an occasion of national (tribal) importance the ancestors must join in making the sacrifice".[390]

[383] Kenyatta, 1938, pp. 171–4; Routledge, 1910, pp. 130-1; Cagnolo, 1933, pp. 113–14; Tate, 2, 1904; Champion, 1912, p. 84.

[384] Kenyatta, 1938, p. 174; Routledge, 1910, p. 131; Cagnolo, 1933, p. 114.

[385] Champion, 1912, p. 86.

[386] Kenyatta, 1938, p. 183.

[387] See below, p. 64.

[388] Hobley, 1938, pp. 97–9; Routledge, 1910, pp. 170–1; Cagnolo, 1933, pp. 143–6; Laughton, 1944, p. 13; Orde-Browne, 1925, pp. 94–5; Champion, 1912, p. 84.

[388a] Routledge, 1910, pp. 168–70; Cagnolo, 1933, p. 142; Orde-Browne, 1925, pp. 94–5.

[389] Hobley, 1938, pp. 94, 98; Routledge, 1910, p. 172; Orde-Browne, 1925, p. 95; Cagnolo, 1933, p. 140.

[390] Hobley, 1938, p. 22; Kenyatta, 1938, p. 233.

The Kikuyu mainly think of life after death as organised on the same lines as life here on earth: all earthly life has its spiritual counterpart and both are connected in the living person or institution.

The soul in life is *ngoro*. The spirit after death is called *ngoma*.[391] Kenyatta states that there are three classes of spirits: (i) those of the father or mother which communicate directly with the living children; (ii) clan spirits; (iii) age-set or "tribal" spirits, concerned with the activities of their particular age-set. "The three groups of spirits, composed of young and old men, women and children, in their respective age-groups, are joined in a wider group. This grouping corresponds to a tribal organization of the spirit world. It directs its activities to the more important matters of the tribe; it is not interested in individuals."[392]

The question of the "tribal" spirits is puzzling, since, as will be seen, sacrifices are not made to the ancestors by representatives of wider groupings than the *mbari* or perhaps the district. There are no other explicit references to them in the literature. There is however some information as to the spirits of individual persons. Each person has one spirit only, and the *ngoma*'s personal attributes are similar to those he possessed while alive.[393] The *ngoma* live underground, in their own world called *miri-ini ya mukongoe*.[394] They also appear in the world of the living. They are especially fond of frequenting the hut in which they formerly dwelt; they may possess cattle, and commonly take the form of certain caterpillars, hyenas, kites, and perhaps snakes and mongooses. They are said to live in sacred fig-trees:[395] it may be that the relationship between them and God can be seen from the fact that both are manifest in these trees. Hobley states that God can control the spirits, since He is often implored to send them away from places where they are troublesome.[396]

There appears to be little or no belief in ancestor spirits among the Northern tribes. Among the Meru ancestor spirits are *nkoro*, and there is a term *nkoma*, used for all types of spirits including *nkoro*. In Embu and Mbere *ngoma* are "devils, evil spirits."[397]

The Kikuyu believe in a God, *Ngai* or *Murungu*. He dwells on certain mountains —Mount Kenya, Kinangop in the Aberdares, Kianjahi in the east and Kiambiruiru in the south, and on Longonot Crater in Masai territory.[398] He also dwells in the sacred fig-trees at which sacrifices are made to him, and His power is manifested in the sun, moon, stars, rain and rainbow, lightning and thunder.[399] He is addressed as *Mwenenyaga* (Possessor of Whiteness).[400] Tate states that there are three Gods, all called *Ngai*: one sends riches, another children and the third misfortune[401]; but these are best regarded as different aspects of the one *Ngai*.

Ngai is the omnipotent creator of the world. The nature of His powers is indicated by the occasions on which prayers and sacrifices are offered to Him. Sacrifices are offered in times of drought, epidemic, and so on, and also at certain points in the agricultural calendar: at planting, when crops begin to grow; and at harvesting.[402]

[391] Routledge, 1910, pp. 239–40; also Hobley, 1938, p. 28.

[392] Kenyatta, 1938, p. 266. See also Cayzac, 1910, p. 310; and Hobley, 1938, p. 28, both of whom state that the spirits of women and children are of significance.

[393] Hobley, 1938, pp. 28–9.

[394] Routledge, 1910, pp. 243–4; Hobley, 1938, p. 28. Routledge states that this is pre-missionary belief.

[395] Routledge, 1910, pp. 240–2; Hobley, 1938, pp. 29–30; Tate, 1910, p. 243. Hyenas and kites are scavengers, and eat corpses; there is a ritual connection between them and *thahu* (ritual uncleanness).

[396] Hobley, 1938, p. 28.

[397] Orde-Browne, 1925, pp. 95–6, 206; Lambert, 1950, pp. 117 ff.

[398] Kenyatta, 1938, p. 236; Routledge, 1910, p. 226; Orde-Browne, 1925, p. 205; Boyes, 1911, p. 261.

[399] Kenyatta, 1938, pp. 236–8; Routledge, 1910, p. 226; Cagnolo, 1933, pp. 27, 196–7; Laughton, 1944, p. 16.

[400] Routledge, 1910, p. 226; Kenyatta, 1938, p. 234. Mount Kenya is called *Kerenyaga*, the place of whiteness. Cf. also the ritual significance of *ira*, the white diatomite powder, which is used in many rites.

[401] Tate, 2, 1904, p. 263.

[402] Kenyatta, 1938, pp. 238–40; Routledge, 1910, p. 227.

Ngai is also approached at the major crises in an individual's life, at the birth, initiation, marriage and death of every Kikuyu. At lesser crises of life communion with the ancestors is sufficient.

The distinction between communion with *Ngai* and with the ancestors is seen most clearly in the differences in the two rituals. The expression used for sacrifice to God is *guthaithaya Ngai*—to beseech God—whereas that for sacrifice to the ancestors in *guitangira ngoma njohi*—to pour out beer for the spirits, or *guthinjira na guitangira ngoma njohi*—to slaughter a goat and pour out beer for the spirits.[403] The persons participating in the two rituals are different and represent different social groupings. Assistance from God is always obtained by the *mbari*.[404] For minor misfortunes *Ngai* is not approached. Purification is carried out by the medicine man, who will establish contact with such of the ancestral spirits as may be thought to be concerned.

The groupings involved in their inter-relationship can be seen from a consideration of the various shrines. Details are confusing, but it is important to clarify the matter since they are the focal points of the various ritual (and political) groupings in Kikuyu society.

The shrines to *Ngai* are the sacred trees or groves called *mugumo*; these are fig-trees, *mukuyu* for the Masai guild and *mutamaiyu* for the Kikuyu guild.[405] Not all fig-trees are sacred.[406] When clearing a field, a large tree is usually left which "is believed to collect the spirits from all other trees which have been cut in the vicinity". If the tree later dies and must be cut, a ram is sacrificed, and the spirits move to another tree. The wood can be used by old people or for honey barrels.[407] A *mugumo* may not be cut down, and is a sanctuary for animals and men.[408]

Beech states definitely that sacrifices at a *mugumo* are to *Ngai* only, there being no trace of any connection with the ancestor cult; the head of the village has a private sacred tree. Dundas equates these trees with the Kamba *ithembo*, to which Hobley gives the two meanings of sacred places "for each big division of the country" for sacrifices to Ngai, and sacred places for a group of two or three villages for sacrifices to the ancestors.[409] It would seem fair to assume that a family group's sacrifices to *Ngai* (and communication with the ancestors) are made at the "private" village trees, and that the community's sacrifices to *Ngai* are made at the "public" trees, "for each big division of the country". Kenyatta says that "a group of families . . . cannot function together except in times of crisis, for each will have its own father", and that the "family group" or *mbari* is the religious unit. When dealing with sacrifices to *Ngai* at times of tribal crisis, he writes: "When all the necessary arrangements have been made, a day is appointed on which the sacrifice is to be offered. The offering is made in all districts and locations simultaneously. Locations are divided by rivers and streams. Thus people between one river and another are considered to constitute a sacrificial unit. They have one sacred tree or grove under which they offer their sacrifice in common".[410] Hobley states that at a sacrifice "the elders of both the circumcision guilds go together to the sacred tree and also elders of all clans". He also implies that the ritual unit is the "ridge".[411] This group is presumably a group larger than the *mbari*.[412] Orde-Browne states that sacred groves exist among the

[403] Kenyatta, 1938, p. 232.

[404] Kenyatta, 1938, p. 309.

[405] Hobley, 1938, p. 49. The actual tree is a parasitical *ficus*; see Beech, 1, 1913, p. 4; Cayzac, 1910, p. 319; Lambert, 1950, p. 21 n.

[406] Barlow, 1915, p. 41.

[407] Hobley, 1938, pp. 31–2; also p. 41.

[408] Routledge, 1910, p. 38; Tate, 1910, p. 242; Tate, 2, 1904, p. 263; Cagnolo, 1933, p. 27; Hobley, 1938, pp. 47–8.

[409] Beech, 1, 1913, p. 5; Hobley, 1938, pp. 40, 48, 53; C. Dundas, 1915, p. 240; Beecher, 1944, p. 15.

[410] Kenyatta, 1938, pp. 235, 245–6.

[411] Hobley, 1938, p. 41; see p. 29 above.

[412] See above, pp. 29.

Northern tribes but that he saw no rites. Among the Tharaka there are ritual places, which link villages: these are trees, rocks and waterfalls, called *iri*; no further details are given. The Mwimbi have a sacred hill called Kiera, on which sacrifices are made.[413] Lambert mentions sacred groves for each generation division of Chuka, Embu and Mbere.[414]

In addition to its sacred tree, each village has an ancestor shrine of three stones.[415] Meat, beer, blood and fat are placed on or poured between the stones, in two portions, one for the male and one for the female ancestors.[416] Presumably these shrines are those referred to above by Hobley, and offerings to the ancestors are made here, as "either a communal or an individual act".

In summary, there appear to be the following categories of sacrifices:

(a) Sacrifice to *Ngai* by the representatives of the local community at the "public" sacred trees.

(b) Sacrifice to *Ngai* by the heads of *mbari* over a wide area, in unison at the "private" trees. The difference between these two categories depends upon the seriousness of the crisis.

(c) Sacrifice to *Ngai* by the representatives of the *mbari* on an occasion affecting the *mbari* only.

(d) Communion with and offerings to the ancestor spirits, which take place at the family shrines of stones, and which also occur at the "private" trees of *mbari*.

Sacrifices to *Ngai* are offered, as has been mentioned, at certain points in the agricultural calendar and also at times of crisis. At such times, the decision to offer a sacrifice is made by a *murathi* or seer, who is an elder of *ukuru* in direct communication with *Ngai* who gives him instructions, generally in dreams. This power may only be used on behalf of the community and never for private gain. A seer is distinct from a medicine man (*mundu mugo*).[417] The participants at such a sacrifice are the elders of *ukuru* and women who are past childbearing; others must stay away from *mugumo*. On the day of sacrifice peace must be kept and no unnecessary journeys made, arms may not be taken to the tree, the ground must not be touched with iron; elders at feud may not participate.[418]

At ceremonies at the "private" trees in each *mbari* area, women and children may attend, although they must stay some way from the tree; for two days before and after the sacrifice the village is in seclusion, no strangers may sleep there and nothing may be taken out.[419]

The head of the family only may sacrifice to the ancestors, usually on the advice of a *mundu mugo* (medicine man). The whole domestic family participates in the ceremony, which centres round the *nyumba*, the wife's hut (presumably in the polygynous family the hut of the senior wife); strangers are not allowed in the village or homestead. Occasions for such an offering are misfortunes, and an elder usually sacrifices to his ancestors every three months.[420]

In addition to sacrifices to *Ngai* and communion with the ancestors, Hobley mentions that at certain rivers passers-by will spit or throw grass into the river. People place stones on a fallen tree, and place grass inside an elephant's skull when found.[421] Routledge describes what he calls a ceremony to do with snake worship: he is actually referring to the rite in the *ituika* ceremony which features the *ndamathia*, or rainbow-serpent.[422]

[413] Orde-Browne, 1925, p. 205; C. Dundas, 1915, p. 240; Gurney, 1929, p. 205.
[414] Lambert, 1956, p. 47.
[415] Hobley, 1938, p. 69.
[416] Hobley, 1938, pp. 70–1. It is not clear from the account whether the two groups of spirits are distinguished by sex, or whether they are the patrilineal and the matrilineal spirits.
[417] Kenyatta, 1938, pp. 242–3; Hobley, 1938, pp. 36–9.
[418] Kenyatta, 1938, pp. 238, 263; Cagnolo, 1933, p. 187; Routledge, 1910, pp. 229–36; Hobley, 1938, pp. 34–5, 42–7; Stigand, 1913, p. 242; von Höhnel, I, 1894, p. 312; C. Dundas, 1921, p. 238.
[419] Routledge, 1910, pp. 229–36; Kenyatta, 1938, pp. 81, 239; Hobley, 1938, pp. 49, 73.
[420] Routledge, 1910, p. 241; Kenyatta, 1938, pp. 77, 114, 266–7; Hobley, 1938, pp. 40, 50–3.
[421] Hobley, 1938, p. 34.
[422] Routledge, 1910, pp. 237–8; see p. 38, above.

Modern Religious Movements

Kikuyu has been the scene of much missionary enterprise and of separatist churches independent of mission control. The earliest of the latter seems to have been formed about 1922 in Fort Hall. After the "circumcision controversy" of the late 1920s the missions lost many of their adherents, and the number of independent churches increased throughout the 1930s. They were mostly ephemeral sects, often advocating polygamy, speaking with tongues, and with strong anti-European sentiments. The best known sects were the *Watu wa Mungu* ("People of God") led by seers (*arathi*), and the later *Dini ya Jesu Kristo* ("Religion of Jesus Christ") formed from the earlier sect. These and the many other similar sects were associated with the independent schools movements, and, according to some writers, with the Mau Mau movement. As yet little is really known about these important politico-religious movements.[423]

Kikuyu "Guilds"

In Kikuyu there is a system of what various writers have called "guilds". Hobley states that "members of the Kikuyu tribes from birth to old age pass through various grades of initiation, but the ceremonial observed is of two classes, one of which is referred to . .. as the Kikuyu system and the other the Masai system".[424] Beecher writes: "There is a division of the tribe into two guilds quite independently of the division into clans and sub-clans . . . membership of one guild or the other determined the customs to be followed (in ritual). The guilds are called respectively the Masai guild and the Kikuyu guilt. . . . Membership of a guild is generally hereditary, although it is not necessary for a son to adhere to the guild to which his father belonged. A man may feel that he should change over from one guild to the other, in order to bring to an end a particularly long run of "bad luck". The changing-over ceremony is a form of "ceremonial purification", and, in a simpler form ". . . is always performed when a girl marries a man of the other guild".[425] The guilds are neither exogamous nor endogamous. Beecher adds that the Masai guild is the smaller and that most of its members live in south-west Kikuyu—that part nearest the Masai. In a case of marriage between members of different guilds it is the woman who changes her guild. The guilds have different rites for Second Birth and initiation and are separated at funerals. The rules concerned *thahu* (ritual uncleanness) differ for each guild.[426]

A Masai or other non-Kikuyu who had become a Kikuyu through "adoption" would always belong to the Masai division with his dependents. He could not change his affiliation. Neither could a Masai woman proper change on marriage to a Kikuyu, nor her descendants. The Masai division seem to have had less stringent rules regarding *thahu*. An individual family within a *mbari* could change, the *mbari* remaining in the original division. More research is still needed but at the moment it seems that the "guilds" had ritual-religious significance and no political implication.

Magic and Sorcery

There are two types of magical practitioner in Kikuyu society, the *mundu mugo* and the *murogi*. The *mundu mugo*[427] is generally referred to in the literature as medicine man, witch-doctor or magician, and *murogi*[428] as wizard or practitioner in

[423] See especially Welbourn 1961, and Rawcliffe 1954; this material is summarized in Middleton, 1965.

[424] Hobley, 1938, p. 77; Beecher, 1944, pp. 5–6.

[425] Beecher, 1944, pp. 5–6

[426] Hobley, 1938, pp. 103 ff. and 70, 86, 100, 106–26.

[427] The literal translation is "clever man", but as Routledge points out, the word *mugo* is also used in connection with the sacred tree, *mugumo* or *muti mugo*; he translates *mundu mugo* as "Man of God" (Routledge, 1910, p. 249).

[428] From *orogi* (poison) (Routledge, 1910, p. 272).

witchcraft. The essential difference is that *murogi* can be a practitioner of harmful magic and sorcery whereas *mundu mugo* practices good or white magic. They are referred to here as medicine man (*mundu mugo*) and sorcerer (*murogi*). The same distinction is found among the Northern tribes, where they are called *mugaa*, *mundu mugo*, and *mganga*.[429]

(*a*) *The mundu mugo*

According to Routledge a medicine man has no official position connected with his special gifts. When he appears in the capacity of a prophet[430] he does so either on his own initiative or in compliance with a generally expressed sentiment that divine guidance should be obtained in reference to the subject in hand. Every valley or petty district has its medicine man, and Routledge estimates that they represent about five per thousand of the total population. "The reputation and prestige enjoyed by different medicine men varies greatly, but the sum of their individual and collective powers in the land is very great. No man otherwise than intelligent would attempt to enter the profession, and if he did he would be refused. The calling is not necessarily a hereditary one, nor does it seem to be associated with the accumulation of great wealth; influence and substantial competency appear to be its general reward."[431]

Routledge adds that a medicine man is "called": he may be taken sick, and his calling is revealed by divination, or he has dreams and visions of God. "A father may teach, but it is God who chooses the medicine man. He talks to him in the night: it comes into his head." If he resists the call God is angry and sends misfortunes on him, his kin and his village. The call comes usually in late middle age. Cayzac states that the profession is often transmitted to sons, although it is not usually hereditary.[432]

A medicine man is initiated by the corporation of medicine men of the district, and in particular by his own sponsor among them. The initiation is public and includes immersion in a river; he is later given medicine gourds and instructed in divination. Irregular practitioners are poisoned.[433]

The medicine man practises for private clients, and his role has three principal aspects: he can purify from *thahu* (ritual uncleanness); he can act as a diviner; he makes charms and medicines and counters disease, he also acts as ritual adviser in the age-set system.

Ritual uncleanness (*thahu*) is generally incurred through the performance, voluntary or involuntary, of certain acts, some of which are inevitable in everyday life. *Thahu* may be caused also by magic or sorcery and by defiance of a parent's instructions.[434] Radcliffe-Browne writes that "the word *thahu* denotes the undesirable ritual status that results from failure to observe rules of ritual avoidance".[435]

Hobley gives sixty-eight examples of *thahu*; the cases vary according to whether a person is a member of the Masai or Kikuyu guild.[436] He points out that in a number of cases the *thahu* is brought upon the offender or upon a third party by the intentional act of the offender; in other cases the *thahu* is the result of circumstances over which there is no control, so that a person can scarcely go through life without becoming *thahu* at some time or other. Unmarried men and girls are not subject to *thahu*.[437]

When *thahu* is incurred purification is necessary. In grave cases the services of a medicine man are needed; less serious cases can be purified by any elder of *ukuru*

[429] Bernardi, 1959, pp. 128 ff.; Orde-Browne, 1925, pp. 182–3; the term *mganga* is suspect, since it is Swahili for "doctor" but no other term is given as being used.
[430] He is not a *murathi* or seer: Routledge may be confused between them.
[431] Routledge, 1910, pp. 249–50; also Tate, 2, 1904, p. 263.
[432] Routledge, 1910, p. 251; Cayzac, 1910, p. 313; Orde-Browne, 1925, pp. 56, 205.
[433] Routledge, 1910, pp. 252–4; Cagnolo, 1933, p. 133.
[434] Hobley, 1938, pp. 103 ff.; he translates *thahu* by "curse" (in its medieval sense); Routledge, 1910, p. 256.
[435] Radcliffe-Brown, 1939, p. 11.
[436] Hobley, 1938, pp. 105 ff.; also Routledge, 1910, pp. 256–8; Cagnolo, 1933, pp. 177–81; 188–9; Orde-Browne, 1925, p. 183; Tate, 2, 1904, p. 264.
[437] Hobley, 1938, pp. 142–3.

who has lost a wife who has borne children. All elders of *ukuru* are partially immune to *thahu*.[438]

Purification is effected by "vomiting the sin". The contents of a goat's stomach (*taatha*) are prepared with medicines. The mixture is placed on the patient's tongue with a brush, and the *thahu* are enumerated. He spits out the *taatha* as they are mentioned. The medicine man also purifies the hut of the patient by brushing the walls with *taatha*; if the *thahu* is not removed in this way the hut may have to be demolished.[439]

The *mundu mugo* generally practises divination on behalf of a private client in case of misfortune or illness, to discover the cause and prescribe the cure. Divination is by means of counters, which are normally carried in a special gourd given to him at his initiation into the corporation.[440]

The *mundu mugo* is also a maker of medicines and of counter-medicines and charms against sorcery. Details of the various medicines and charms made by the *mundu mugo* are given by various writers.[441]

The medicine man's treatment of disease is based on the notion that the magica root of the disease can be cast out by magical treatment and by purification. The Kikuyu also practise surgery to cure obvious physical wounds. Surgery is not associated with medicine, the domain of the *mundu mugo*, but is practised by anyone with the necessary skill. It is confined to the treatment of flesh wounds (wounds are stitched with thorns) and does not extend to bone-setting or any deeper treatment. For dental decay a tooth is removed by breaking away the socket-wall.[442]

Among the Meru tribes the functionary known as the *mugwe* traditionally exercised a central ritual and spiritual role. He acted as a prophet and diviner, and played an important part in the initiation rites. His influence is today much decreased.[443]

(*b*) *The murogi* (*sorcerer*)

Urogi is poison, not mere "medicine", and is used exclusively for nefariou purposes. According to Kenyatta, the formulae for manufacturing and administerin *urogi* are the property of the sorcerers' secret council, *njama ya arogi*. He describe their secret meetings, held at night, at which the sorcerers are unknown to each other and adds that the people of a district where such a group is known to exist are in suc terror that the matter cannot be discussed. A *murogi*, in order to conceal his nefariou activities, practises as an ordinary *mundu mugo*.[444]

Urogi comes from outside Kikuyu: both the Kamba and Tharaka are renowne for the power of their bad medicines.[445]

Certain clans are known to possess magical powers: the Aithaga clan is divide into two divisions, the members of one having powers of rain-making and those of th other powers of sorcery. No *mundu mugo* can remove a spell imposed by a Mwaithaga howeevr, a Mwaithaga is liable to *thahu*. The Aceera and Anjiru clans are noted fc their power of the evil eye, although this may be possessed by members of othe clans.[446]

Magical powers are also possessed by smiths. A smith can inflict *thahu*, can pu a curse on a trespasser, and alone can purify a man so cursed. A smith protects hi own property by placing old bellows-nozzles on it. Smiths were sometimes employe

[438] Hobley, 1938, pp. 104–5, 126–7; 1910, p. 440; Routledge, 1910, p. 256; Cagnolo, 193 pp. 188–9; Crawford, 1903, p. 54; Orde-Browne, 1925, pp. 52, 181.

[439] Routledge, pp. 258–63; Hobley, 1938, pp. 135–7, 144 (a slightly different account Cayzac, 1910, p. 311; Crawford, pp. 54–5; Boyes, 1911, p. 258.

[440] Routledge, pp. 263–8; his account includes a description of the counters and the significance; Cagnolo, 1933; pp. 134–5; Crawford, p. 54; Orde-Browne, 1925, pp. 185–6.

[441] Routledge, pp. 250, 276–9; Cagnolo, pp. 131–5, 181–4; Hobley, 1938, pp. 184–9 194–8; Hobley, 1906; Tate, 2, 1904, p. 262; Bugeau, 1943, p. 201; Orde-Browne, 1925, p 202–3; Champion, p. 83, Stigand, p. 252.

[442] Routledge, 1910, pp. 33, 280.

[443] Bernardi, 1959, *passim*.

[444] Kenyatta, 1938, pp. 299–301, 306–7; Routledge, pp. 272–4.

[445] Boyes, 1911, p. 119; Champion, p. 90.

[446] Hobley, 1938, pp. 177–83.

to settle law-cases, on account of their power to curse evil-doers.[447] The Aithaga can never become smiths, and they must avoid each other.[448]

Myths and Cosmology

Myths of origin of the Kikuyu are given by Routledge[449]; other myths and fables are given by various writers.[450] Cagnolo lists some Kikuyu proverbs[451], and gives a short account of Kikuyu cosmological beliefs and time-reckoning.[452] Myths of origin are given in detail for the Meru tribes by Bernardi.[453]

II. THE KAMBA

Tribal and Sub-tribal Groupings

Nomenclature and Location

The Kamba[454] inhabit the present-day administrative districts of Machakos and Kitui, the River Athi being their common boundary; Machakos contains the traditional sections of Ulu and Kikumbuliu or Kibwezi, and Kitui contains the sections of Kitui and Mumoni. Slight cultural and dialectal differences are recognized between the divisions, but the Kamba consider themselves to be one people. The people of Ulu ("the high country") sometimes refer to those of Kitui as Adaisu or Athaisu.

Other groups of Kamba, numbering several thousands, live outside UKamba, in Rabai near Mombasa, in Teita and Digo, in the area between Lake Jipe and Taveta and still farther south in central Tanganyika.[455] Some of these groups are thought to have emigrated in order to escape famine, which was formerly frequent; contact was maintained with the parent groups, particularly by the group of Rabai which had strong trading connections with the inland Kamba.[456]

The Kamba are said to have been called *Lung'u* by the Masai[457] and *Wamanguo* (from *nguo*, "clothes") or *Waringao* by the Swahili, the term meaning "the naked people".[458]

Kamba country is today bounded on the south by the line of the railway from Mombasa to Nairobi (with Kikumbuliu as an enclave to the south of the line), the border running from the station of Mtito Andei to Kiu; to the west the boundary runs from Kiu to the north where the boundary is the Tana River as far as the northern tip of the Mumoni range. North-east and east the country is almost desert, and there is no clear boundary. Most of the population is to the west, in Ulu.

Neighbouring Peoples

To the west are the Kikuyu, and to the north-west the Tharaka and Mbere, all related peoples. To the south-west are the Masai, with whom there was constant raiding. Kikumbuliu adjoins the Teita hills. To the north-east and east are the Boran Galla, with whom there was also constant raiding, the Pokomo and various small nomadic groups known as Boni and Sanye (or Arangulo).[459]

[447] Hobley, 1938, pp. 169–73; Kenyatta, pp. 75–; Cagnolo, p. 188; Laughton, 1944, p. 8; Routledge, p. 91; Orde-Browne, 1925, p. 131; Boyes, p. 246.

[448] Hobley, 1938, pp. 165, 182.

[449] Routledge, 1910, pp. 283–4.

[450] Routledge, pp. 285–328; Cagnolo, 1932, pp. 226–46; Hobley, 1938, pp. 262–5; Barrett, *passim*; Orde-Browne, 1925, pp. 209–18; Beecher, 1938.

[451] Cagnolo, pp. 214–25; Dougall, 1928.

[452] Cagnolo, pp. 191–9.

[453] Bernardi, 1959, 52–75; see also Needham, 1960.

[454] The correct designation for persons is Mukamba in the singular and AKamba in the plural; the country is UKamba and the language KiKamba. The term Kamba will be used for both noun and adjective.

[455] Beidelman, 1961.

[456] Lindblom, 1920, pp. 10, 571–2; Krapf, 1860, p. 197; Kenya Land Commission Evidence, 1932, II, p. 1,300; Prins, 1952, p. 39; Johnstone, 1902, pp. 263, 268.

[457] Hobley (1910, p. 3) gives Kamba names for other peoples.

[458] Lindblom, 1920, pp. 22, 573.

[459] Lindblom, 1920, pp. 17 ff.

DEMOGRAPHY[460]

The populations of the two main Kamba Districts in 1948 were:

District	*Population*	*Tribe*
Machakos	350,866	Kamba
Kitui	203,035	Kamba
	5,101	Meru

There were in Kenya as a whole in 1948 a total of 389,777 Machakos Kamba and 221,948 Kitui Kamba. Besides those given above, Kamba were living in other Districts elsewhere in Kenya, as follows:

Nairobi, 7,829; Thika, 21,395; Mombasa, 5,137; Kwale, 2,243; Kilifi, 2,189; Kajiado, 1,034.

TRADITIONS OF ORIGIN AND HISTORY

The Kamba were apparently once a compact group occupying the region now called Ulu, and they consider the Mbooni Mountains as the point from which they settled Kitui and the other areas. There are traditions that they came to Ulu either from the Giriama country near the coast or from the neighbourhood of Kilimanjaro. They consider themselves to have been a hunting and agricultural people who learnt about cattle on trading expeditions and bought them with ivory.[461]

Lindblom dates the crossing of the River Athi and the settlement of Kitui from Ulu in the first half of the eighteenth century. They expanded throughout all Ulu and into Kikumbuliu during the nineteenth century.[462]

The Imperial British East Africa Company opened a station at Machakos in 1892 and a few years later the first Indian-owned stores was opened and the use of currency was introduced. The company laid down its charter in 1895 and a protectorate over British East Africa was declared, the administration being taken over by the Foreign Office and later by the Colonial Office. A police post was set up at Kitui in 1893, its main purpose being to check slave caravans, but European administration did not begin till 1898.[463]

The building of the Kenya and Uganda Railway, which was a great factor in establishing effective control and has obviously influenced economic affairs, was begun in 1896. The first white settlers received grants of land in 1903, chiefly British and Dutch from South Africa, and in 1948 there were 313 Europeans living in Ukamba.[464] Many Kamba work on European farms and in the towns.

Missions working among the Kamba are Seventh Day Adventists and the Africa Inland Mission.[465]

LANGUAGE

The Kamba speak one language, but there are considerable differences of vocabulary and construction between the dialects of Machakos and Kitui, the latter dialect sometimes being called Daisu or Thaisu.[466] There are minor differences between Kitui and Mumoni, and between Ulu and Kibwezi.[467]

The phonetic and grammatical characteristics of Kamba are given by Guthrie and Doke.[468] The latter also gives a bibliography of grammars and dictionaries. It belongs to Doke's "Northern Bantu" zone and to Guthrie's "Zone E, group 50", which includes Kikuyu, Embu and Meru.

Swahili is the usual *lingua franca* between Kamba and Europeans or Indians. English is becoming fairly common, especially in Machakos District.

[460] From 1948 Census figures.
[461] Lindblom, 1920, pp. 349–50, 476; Larby, 1944, p. 25; K.L.C. Evidence, 1932, II, p. 1,285
[462] Lindblom, 1920, p. 10; K.L.C. Evidence, II, p. 1,295.
[463] Lindblom, 1920, pp. 352, 579; Larby, p. 25; Stanner, 1939, Section II.
[464] E. African Statistical Department, Preliminary Estimates of the Civil Non-Nativ[e] Population, 1948, Table 5.
[465] Philp, 1936.
[466] Lindblom, 1920, p. 15.
[467] Stanner, personal communication.
[468] Guthrie, 1948, pp. 43–5; Doke, 1945, p. 15.

PHYSICAL ENVIRONMENT

The Kamba live on the eastern slopes of the Kikuyu highlands, which fall gradually from a height of about 5,000 feet at Machakos to some 1,500 feet on the eastern boundary, where the country joins the northern part of the Nyika desert, inland from the coast. Ecological factors vary widely. In Machakos it was estimated in 1932 that of a total of 1,400,000 acres, about 140,000 were cultivated, 70,000 lying fallow, and 200,000 or 300,000 acres uninhabited owing to tsetse.[469] Of the non-tsetse areas, much consists of steep hill-sides, rocky and sandy country; to the east the country is almost waterless, and in Kikumbuliu the only sources of water are a few streams in the Chyulu Hills and the taps at railway stations, which are used for humans and livestock as well as for railway engines.[470] Large parts of the country have been described as "little more than a scrub-covered desert, slowly deteriorating through over-population".[471] In Kitui most of the population live along the few rivers, and Dundas states that he saw villages as much as seven hours' march from water.[472]

MAIN FEATURES OF ECONOMY

Agriculture, Livestock and Diet

The Kamba make their fields along the banks of rivers, in small depressions and other well-watered places, where possible. They know how to irrigate their fields by ditches.[473]

Traditionally the main crops are sorghum, maize and millet. The most popular legume is pigeon pea, and there are other types of beans and peas. Sweet potatoes, yams and manioc are common. Sugar-cane is grown on low ground, in some parts in pits in valleys, and bananas are grown in several varieties. Crops are usually grown in mixed stands.[474]

The Kamba have considerable numbers of cattle, sheep and goats, the cattle being a short-horned zebu type. Herds are usually dispersed for grazing among widely separated kraals. There is some seasonal cattle movement into the semi-desert areas of the east from Kitui.[475]

The diet is mainly vegetarian. Meat of both domestic and game animals is eaten, as are grasshoppers and other insects. Milk and butter are both used as food, the latter also being used as a toilet grease.[476] Much honey is eaten, and beer made from sugar-cane or honey is drunk: the fermenting agent is the fruit of *kigelia*.[477]

Trade

The Kamba were famous traders, trade being of great economic importance for them. Low has suggested that their dependence on trade was largely due to their proneness to famine, and points out that the Kamba were the only tribe of Kenya to dominate all the three processes of trade between the interior and the Coast—collection, transporting and final export.[478] The main commodity was ivory, but foodstuffs and sometimes slaves were also traded. Even today, the Kamba organize trade in wood carvings as far as England and the United States.[479]

Trade was important between Kamba and Arab and Swahili caravans, many of which reached Ukamba, although they were rarely allowed to enter the country. The Kamba traded in ivory and slaves, among other commodities: a small trade in slaves was going on during Lindblom's visit in 1911–12. Part of this trade in ivory

469 K.L.C. Report, 1932, paras. 725, 730.
470 K.L.C. Evidence, 1932, II, p. 1,305.
471 Larby, 1944, p. 2.
472 C. Dundas, 1913, pp. 480, 495, 500.
473 Lindblom, 1920, pp. 501–2; Hobley, 1910, p. 20.
474 Lindblom, 1920, pp. 505–6; Hobley, 1910, p. 21; both give lists of crops.
475 Lindblom, 1920, pp. 477 ff.; K.L.C. Report, 1932, para. 746; Hildebrandt, 1878, pp. 380–1.
476 Lindblom, 1920, pp. 511 ff.
477 Lindblom, 1920, pp. 518 ff.; Hobley, 2, 1910, p. 31; Thorp, 1943.
478 Low, 1963, pp. 314–15; Wakefield, 1870.
479 Elkan, 1958.

was between the coast and farther inland, the Kamba acting as middlemen. There was also some trade in tobacco.[480]

Lambert stated that large markets were common, attended by people from a wide area.[481]

Crafts

(a) *Hut-building*

A description of the homestead is given by Lindblom. Huts are different from those of the Kikuyu, the framework consisting of young trees placed in a circle in the ground and joined at the top by twigs placed crosswise and forming concentric circles. The roof is thatched, and there is a strong centre-post. Inside there is a partitioned sleeping-place. The central point of the hut is the fireplace of three stones. Fire is only made in a new hut; otherwise it is brought in from a nearby homestead. In a new hut, fire is made after all iron objects have been removed; the inhabitants eat a ceremonial meal and on the second night the husband and wife have ritual intercourse. Hut-building for a medicine man has certain variations.[482]

Near the hut are the granaries, one for each wife; in Kikumbuliu the granaries are in the fields. Construction is of the same type of that of the hut. Different grains are kept in individual containers made of grass coated with dung and placed inside the granaries.

(b) *Agricultural implements*

The principal implement is the wooden digging-stick. Fields are first cleared with iron knives.[483]

(c) *Traps*

The Kamba use many kinds of traps, both for animals and birds.[484]

(d) *Weapons*

Kamba weapons are bow and arrow, sword and clubs; they do not use spears or shields. Arrows are of various types, and in Ulu bear clan marks; poison is used. The bow is the plain straight-staved bow.[485]

(e) *Wooden implements*

The Kamba use wood for stools, snuff-bottles, bee-boxes, which are marked with clan marks, musical instruments (see below), household furniture, pipes, etc. Wood is carved with axe, adze and knife.[486] The Kamba are noted for their wood-carving and are found as itinerant wood-carvers throughout East Africa today.

(f) *Pottery*

Pottery (used only for cooking) is made by women specialists; there is one clan whose women are prohibited from pot-making. The material used is a mixture of black and red clays. Pots often bear the "trade-mark" of an individual potter; they are made by the coil method and are fired. There are certain observances with regard to new pots and pot-making.[487]

[480] Lindblom, 1920, pp. 12–13, 351 ff., 526; Hildebrandt, 1878, pp. 384–5.
[481] Lambert, 2, 1947, p. 137.
[482] Lindblom, 1920, pp. 432 ff., 436 ff., 445, 505; also C. Dundas, 1913, pp. 492 ff. See also Hobley, 2, 1910, p. 30 (who differs in detail).
[483] Lindblom, 1920, pp. 502–3; C. Dundas, 1913, pp. 495–6; Hobley, 1910, p. 20.
[484] Described by Lindblom, 1920, pp. 469 ff. (illus.); Hobley, 1910, pp. 30 ff.
[485] Lindblom, 1920, pp. 499 ff. (illus., great details), pp. 132 ff.; Hobley, 1910, pp. 43 ff.; Johnstone, 1902, p. 270.
[486] Lindblom, 1920, pp. 129 ff., 139 ff., 354 ff., 399 (illus.), 494 ff., 522 ff., 534 ff. (illus.); Hobley, 1910, pp. 33 ff., 40 (illus.); 1922, p. 254 (illus.); Thorp, 1943.
[487] Lindblom, 1920, pp. 536 ff., 155; Hobley, 1910, p. 30.

(*g*) *Gourds and calabashes*

These are used for water, milk and beer and also in divination; they are often elaborately decorated.[488]

(*h*) *String and bag-making*

Bags are made of string prepared from certain barks.[489]

(*i*) *Iron-making*

Iron is used for the implements and weapons already listed, and for making chain, for which the Kamba are famous, and for personal ornaments. Iron is found in river beds and also, apparently, in the form of nuggets of ore, on the ground. Smelting and forging are done by men only. The tools used are bellows, consisting of two sacks of sheepskin, hammers, tongs and pincers.[490]

Music and Dances

Kamba musical instruments consist of drums (both single and double membrane, and a type played by knocking on the ground), musical bows (single-string with calabash resonator), horns, side-blown trumpet, flutes (one type with a reed), rattles and bells.[491] Many dance-drums are elaborately decorated.

There are dances performed by men, by women, by unmarried youths and girls, and by married men and women, on various occasions (birth, wedding, death, harvest, etc.) and at spirit possession and circumcision rites.[492] "Possession" dances are a feature of the Kamba.[493]

Games

Lindblom gives a full description of competitive, gambling, and imitative games, toys, dolls and riddles.[494]

Distribution of Labour

A long list of men's and women's work is given by Lindblom.[495] It is similar to that given above for the Kikuyu,[496] except that Kamba women milk the cows and churn butter.

SOCIAL ORGANIZATION AND POLITICAL SYSTEM

Kinship System

Differing lists of kinship terms are given by Lindblom and Hobley,[497] but according to Stanner the Kamba kinship system is similar to that of the Kikuyu.[498] Some of the terms are the same. There are presumably differences between the terms used in Ulu and Kitui, which may explain some of the discrepancies between the accounts.

Fictional Kinship

Sworn brotherhood is a form of relationship which exists both internally in Ukamba and also between the Kamba and members of other tribes. In both cases the essential ceremony consists in each person consuming a little of the other's blood.[499]

488 Lindblom, 1920, pp. 259, 357 ff. (illus.), 512, 538; Hobley, 1910, p. 30.

489 Lindblom, 1920, pp. 540 ff. (illus.).

490 Lindblom, 1920, pp. 528 ff., 530 (illus.); also giving details of position of smiths; Hobley, 1910, p. 29.

491 Lindblom, 1920, pp. 398 ff. (illus.), 412.

492 Lindblom, 1920, pp. 407 ff.; C. Dundas, 1913, pp. 508–10.

493 See below, p. 87.

494 Lindblom, 1920, pp. 418 ff. (illus.); Hobley, 1910, pp. 54 ff., 7, 1912.

495 Lindblom, 1920, pp. 543–5.

496 See above, pp. 20–1.

497 Lindblom, 1920, pp. 98 ff.; Hobley, 1910, pp. 50–1; see also Lindblom, 1920, pp. 89–98, and Penwill, 1950, pp. 110–13, for description of affinal relationship and avoidances.

498 Stanner, personal communication.

499 Lindblom, 1920, p. 140.

It is considered to be equally important and of the same nature as siblinghood; there are equally strong obligations to mutual assistance and their children are considered as closely related as are the children of brothers; e.g. marriage between them would be regarded as incestuous. The relationship of blood-brothers to other members of each other's clan is not defined. They have protection when travelling through each other's country and a man may have several along a trading route. To ignore the obligations assumed is expected to result in misfortune and death: the bond cannot be severed, even by mutual agreement. Another form of "brotherhood" may be begun in order to avoid a particular danger. A man in fear of his life may force obligations of friendship upon his enemy if he could suck at the breast of his enemy's wife or daughter.[500] Again the relationship is binding upon the children, between whom marriage is forbidden though sexual intercourse is not.

There is a third type which differs in that it can be broken by either party without the consent or knowledge of the other, by a rite which consists in the smashing of a special pot.[501]

Lambert suggests that there is a special joking relationship between Kamba and the Nyamwezi, but this is not mentioned by Meinhard or Moreau.[502]

Clan System

The Kamba are divided into about 25 dispersed patrilineal totemic clans, varying greatly in size and generally named after the founding ancestor, or some distinguishing characteristic or experience of his. A few exceptions, which may be immigrant groups from Meru or Tharaka, are not dispersed. The coherence of the clan may be maintained by inter-visiting even though it is spread over a wide area, and members speak of ties maintained between Kitui, Machakos and Rabai.[503]

Several clans are considered by the Kamba to be linked or identifiable with certain Kikuyu clans, some of which have a similar name or totem.[504] Lists of clan names and their totems are given by Lindblom, Hobley and Lambert.[505]

There is no specific term for "clan". An agnatic descent group is referred to as *mbai*, regardless of order or size, although *mbai* generally applies to a group larger than the core of the *muvia*, a three- or four-generation joint family.[506] Also a descent group may be designated by the use of the collective prefix *mbaa-*, "the descendants of ——", e.g., *mbaa-Awini* or *mbaa Mbiti*, *mbiti* (the hyena) being the totem of the Awini clan. *Mbaa-* is also used to designate the agnatic core of a *muvia* or joint family, and is also applied to the joint family as a group, e.g., *mbaa-Mbeke*, where Mbeke is the name of the founding ancestor.[507]

Clan members have common totemic observances and duties of assistance towards each other, particularly in litigation and, in cases of homicide, to exact blood-vengeance. They will share the indemnification accepted for the death or the fine imposed for a lesser offence, and if a clan member is the wrongdoer will contribute to the payment required. The effective group is, however, limited by territorial dispersal. The clan is exogamous and sexual intercourse between members is incestuous, necessitating a purificatory ceremony, unless the relationship between the two groups concerned is so remote that other obligations are no longer considered binding. In such a case a new clan is regarded as having been founded. Dancing together is forbidden to clan members, probably because dances usually end in general sexual intercourse.[508] A man visiting a fellow clansman might be "lent" one

[500] Lindblom, 1920, pp. 141–2.
[501] Hildebrandt, 1878, p. 386.
[502] Lambert, 2, 1947, p. 141; Meinhard, "The Nyamwezi" (unpublished MS.); Moreau, 1941.
[503] Lambert, 2, 1947, p. 133; Lindblom, 1920, pp. 131 ff.; Hobley, 1910, pp. 5–6; C. Dundas, 1913; Larby, 1944, p. 7; K.L.C. Evidence, II, p. 292.
[504] Lindblom, 1920, p. 126; Lambert, 2, 1947, p. 133.
[505] Lindblom, 1920, p. 136 Hobley, 1910, p. 4; Lambert, 2, 1947, p. 132.
[506] Here used for either joint or extended family. See above, p. 25.
[507] Lindblom, 1920, p. 114; Lambert, 2, 1947, p. 163.
[508] Lindblom, 1920, pp. 121–3.

of his host's wives for the duration of his stay, a form of hospitality seldom extended to unrelated friends.[509]

A man can be adopted into a clan, taking upon himself all the obligations of membership, including those of exogamy. The applicant and the head of the *muvia* (joint family) swear an oath on the *kithitu*.[510] Expulsion from the clan is impossible, but a clan member who incurs public disapprobation may be driven away by ostracism.[511]

Each joint family has a cattle brand, *Kyoo*, from which the clan of the owner can be known. Each clan has also a mark for arrowheads. A man may alter his *Kyoo* and take a new one, perhaps that of his mother's kin, if he has consistent misfortune with his cattle, so that in practice confusion may arise. Dundas suggests that the brand is used only on cattle received as part of marriage payments, so that the animals may be traced in case of dispute.[512]

Each dispersed clan has a totem. The list given by Hobley differs markedly from those of Lindblom and Lambert in that it frequently mentions parts of animals, such as lungs or liver, and it seems likely that his questions were misunderstood. For example, a member of the Asii clan, whose totem is the lion, does not eat liver, not because it is his totem, but because the lion is thought never to eat the liver of his prey.

A man will neither kill nor eat his totem animal,[513] nor touch it if he finds it dead, but there are no totemic rituals. The totem is regarded as a clan member but not as the founding ancestor, and is given the same respect and protection as any other clan member; an animal caught in a trap, though ordinarily regarded as a pest, will be freed by a fellow clansman. The animal's temperament and characteristics are thought to be shared by the human members of the clan. The totem animal is well disposed towards his human kin, and will assist them by hunting for them.

Totemic observances have declined very much under modern conditions and today many Kamba cannot name their totem.[514]

Certain clans are also distinguished by non-totemic peculiarities and observances. The Anziu clan are all considered to possess the evil eye. They were called upon to perform a ceremony involving human sacrifice if the normal rain control by the Ambua clan proved ineffective. Members of the Asii clan are thought to be able to heal burns; women of the Akithumbe clan are not allowed to make pottery, usually women's work.[515]

Territorial System

The smallest unit is the *musyi* (pl. *misyi*) or homestead. A *musyi* is the home of an elementary, a compound, or a three- or four-generation joint or extended family. There is usually a stockade round the home of each married man, which contains the huts of his wives, and round the whole homestead. The joint or extended family is called *muvia*, the word for the entrance in the stockade round the *musyi* of this group. It would seem that the component homesteads of an extended family *musyi* are also called *misyi*. The unit generally referred to in the literature as the basic political unit is the *thome*. Outside the entrance to the homestead of a joint family there is a shaded open space, called *thome*, where men sit and discuss everyday events. A *thome* may be shared by several joint families or smaller homesteads, and would seem to be used in a political sense as referring to a group based on an extended family with attached households, which may be of different clan affiliations.

[509] Hobley, 1910, p. 64.
[510] See below, p. 76.
[511] Lindblom, 1920, pp. 126, 161.
[512] Lindblom, 1920, pp. 129 ff.; Hobley, 1910, p. 22; C. Dundas, 1921, p. 256.
[513] The totem animal may be killed if it is preying on a clan member, his crops or his cattle. The normal sanction is fear of the death or sickness of the man or his cattle. Lindblom, 1920, p. 119.
[514] Lambert, 2, 1947, p. 131.
[515] Lindblom, 1920, pp. 123–5; Lambert, 2, 1947, p. 136.

Indeed the component homesteads making up a *thome* may not even be in sight of one another.[516]

Joint families are grouped into wider units, known as *utui* (pl. *motui*) and *kivalo* (pl. *ivalo*). In both cases grouping is on the basis of territorial propinquity, and both contain families of different clan affiliations. An *utui* is a self-contained unit, with its own men's club (*kisuka*), "recreation ground" (*kituto*), elders' council (*nzama*), "bench of magistrates" (*nzili*), war leaders (*athiani*) and place of worship (*kitunyeo kya ng'ondu*). These institutions may be shared by neighbouring *motui*.[517]

The larger group, within which social intercourse, especially intermarriage, is pronounced enough to create a sense of unity, is the *kivalo*. Formerly a fighting unit was based upon it, and it has a common dancing-ground (*ngoma*) and a common place of worship (*ithembo*). A number of *ivalo* might unite in war, the warriors from each swearing an oath of allegiance to their new comrades, but this alliance lasted only for the duration of the fighting and the unit of alliance had no name. There is some indication that intra-*kivalo* links must be fairly permanent, since a man may disperse his wives and cattle over several *motui*: for this to occur there must presumably be a tie strong enough to prevent internal warfare. The difference between *utui* and *kivalo* is not well defined.[518]

A wider area has no generic name, but is referred to as *nthi*, which means "country". An *nthi* may have a specific name, but no social institution belonging to it, except those created by the British administration.[519] However, age-grades and age-sets are common to all *ivalo*, styles of teeth-chipping spread across wider areas, and occasional prophets have arisen to unify wider groupings.[520]

Age-grade System[521]

There are institutionalized age-grades among the Kamba, the more senior of which have political and ritual functions, but they are not connected with initiation-sets, nor is there any system of generation-sets as among the Kikuyu.

A male child is known as *kaana* (a term which includes *kakenge*, an unweaned child, and *kavisi*, a weaned child who can walk); *kivisi* denotes an uncircumcised boy who can herd goats; *kamwana*, a circumcised boy who is old enough to dance but has not yet reached puberty. After puberty he may become *mwanake* (pl. *aanake*), a warrior; he may marry and have children, but may not drink beer. Later he becomes *nthele*, a married man with children who no longer dances, and pays a fee of one to three goats to the *anthele* on being promoted. There are various types of warrior, differentiated by the role played in warfare.

A man then enters into the elders' grades, of which there are three. Lowest are the *atumia ma kisuka*, the elders of *kisuka*, Lambert's "junior club": their duty is to take part in discussion to do with war, peace and communal execution.[522] They also are responsible for the disposal of corpses. They pay ten goats or one bullock to the next higher grade on entering *kisuka*.

The top two grades of elders form the *nzama*, the administrative council of the *utui*, which Lambert calls the "men's senior club". These two grades are the *atumia ma nzama* and the *atumia ma ithembo*. The highest grade apparently forms the *nzili* or inner council. Their special duties are sacerdotal. They pass first through the sub-grade of *aanake ma ithembo*—novices who attend the rituals but play no

[516] This short summary is the only description of the settlement pattern which subsumes all the accounts without mutual inconsistency. See Lindblom, 1920, p. 431 ff. (with diagrams); C. Dundas, 1913, p. 492; 1915, p. 239; Lambert, 2, 1947, p. 139.

[517] Lambert, 2, 1947, pp. 134, 139; Hobley, 1922, p. 174, calls *athiani* "leaders of hunting parties".

[518] Lambert, 2, 1947, pp. 134 ff.; Lindblom, 1920, pp. 201, 466; Dundas, 1915, p. 240.

[519] The modern units of administration are generally wider than *ivalo*.

[520] Lambert, 2, 1947, pp. 135 ff.; C. Dundas, 1913, p. 498; 1915, pp. 240, 258; Lindblom, 1920, p. 176. Such a prophet was the famous Kivoi, the friend of the missionary Krapf.

[521] Hobley, 1910, pp. 49–50; 1922, pp. 218–21; Lindblom, 1920, pp. 143–8; Lambert, 2, 1947, pp. 135, 140; Penwill, 1950, pp. 96–7.

[522] See below, p. 76.

part in them. These grades are common to all Kamba, but the councils operate within the *utui*.

The council sits in an incomplete circle, the most senior member at one end of the line and the most junior at the other. Rank within it is dependent upon the payment of fees and a vacant position in the series, occasioned by the death or retirement of an elder. When a man has become the most senior member any further promotion puts him right outside the circle, and if he attends meetings he must sit behind the other members. A man is forced to retire from his position if he has a son also a member of the *nzama*, whose payments have entitled him to the place next but one to his father; a further payment on the part of the son would seat them next to each other, an intolerable idea to the Kamba. The authorities state that among these elders are often young men, and some old men are not elders; not everyone can enter the highest grade. A son cannot belong to the highest grade unless his father has retired on account of age. An elder of *ithembo* is the custodian of an *ithembo* (place of sacrifice) and a man inherits the custodianship from his father no matter how young he may be: but he cannot sacrifice while his father is alive. It seems probable that in fact the elders of *ithembo* are the heads of component groupings of the *utui* and *kivalo*; there is some confusion in the material between these groups and the *kitunyeo* and *ithembo* connected with them. The assumption may fairly be made that admission to at least the highest grade is in reality conferred on genealogical grounds as among the Kikuyu; more research is needed on this point, which is essential to our understanding of the age-grade system of these peoples.[523]

There are certain elders with ritual powers who are discussed below (p. 86).

There are grades for women, but except for the *iveti sya ithembo* or *iveti sya nzama* (wives of *ithembo* or *nzama*), who take part in sacrifices at *ithembo*, they are not institutionalized.[524]

Legal Procedure and Local Government

Authority within the homestead (*musyi*) occupied by the joint family is vested in the family head who, in theory, has complete control over all members of the group, including adult males with families of their own. It is apparently very common for men to hive off from these groups, especially when the head of the joint family stands in the relationship of a brother. The *musyi* is the land-holding group and the group which seeks vengeance for offences committed against its members, if indemnification is refused.[525]

The main political unit is the *utui*, the territorial cluster of joint families, the unit of the *nzama*. The *nzama* includes all elders (*atumia*) but not all go regularly or take part in its deliberations. Those who do so are called *asili*, or men skilled in law. Any man of wealth or personality may attract followers and be called *munene* (big man) but he will play no part in the government of the area. An elder of great legal wisdom may represent his *utui* in external cases, and is called *mwalania* or *musili*.[526]

All authorities except Hobley agree that the institution of chiefship is alien to the Kamba. The early "chiefs", such as Kivoi, mentioned in some reports, seem rather to have been important traders or prophets.

Members of the elders' council are arbitrators, who have been called upon by the claimants to assess the admitted damage suffered by the appellants and to give their opinion on the compensation due in the particular circumstances. Offences considered are treated as private delicts. In general if a man appears at the *nzama* to defend himself it is a tacit admission of liability, because a claim entirely repudi-

523 This is a summary of several often conflicting accounts: Hobley, 1910, pp. 49–50; 1922, pp. 218–25; Lambert, 2, 1947, pp. 135 ff.; Lindblom, 1920, pp. 143 ff., 220; C. Dundas, 1913, p. 540; 1915, pp. 241–2, 248; Larby, 1944, p. 3.

524 Hobley, 1910, p. 49; Lindblom, 1920, p. 147; Lambert, 2, 1947, p. 165.

525 Lindblom, 1920, p. 149; C. Dundas, 1915, p. 239; K.L.C. Evidence, II, p. 1, 292.

526 Lambert, 2, 1947, pp. 134, 139, 141.

ated is ignored. If a man does deny the charges made, the disputed facts are not discussed by the elders but are left to supernatural powers, one or both of the parties and possibly witnesses submitting to ordeals or taking an oath of innocence; in the latter the case has to be shelved until the oath has had time to work, usually six months. Claims never lapse and are inherited by a man's heirs; and they can never fail merely for lack of evidence; little attention is paid to the evidence of witnesses, for neighbours and clansmen, who are bound to mutual assistance, construe their obligations to include false witness. The basic principle of Kamba law is that of compensation, not punishment or reformation. According to Dundas, the underlying sanction is the fear that if the offender refuses to pay compensation the injured party's joint family will seek physical revenge, taking what they consider rightfully theirs or killing in the case of homicide; sometimes they refuse to accept indemnification, preferring vengeance. There is also a supernatural sanction in the ceremonial curse of the elders, which they can lay upon defaulters, bringing disease and misfortune. The family head is responsible for offences committed by his dependents.[527]

In Machakos the members of the *kisuka* were empowered to execute the decisions of the *nzama* and could impound a defaulter's property.[528]

Ordeals are conducted by a medicine man, *mundu mue*. The commonest is *kivyu*, in which the litigants both lick a red-hot knife blade, which has been smeared with a white powder and is believed to harm only the guilty. All the ordeals follow the same general pattern of discriminating injury, whatever the particular form. Others are ordeal by fire, needle, removing objects from boiling water, the bead in the eye and poison.

The most important oath is that of *kithitu* (or *muma*, according to Lindblom and Penwill), which is ordered by the elders in cases of disputes or disagreement on matters of fact; refusal to take it is regarded as an admission of guilt, and false witness is considered to lead to the certain death of the swearer, his wife or eldest son. A *kithitu* is an object owned by some person who either bought it, generally from the Tharaka, or inherited it, and he receives a fee when it is used. They vary in the strength of their power. Some are earthenware balls, others are horns or tusks and they contain various small objects. They may not rest on the ground nor be touched by the hands unless first anointed with red ochre, and a traveller will make a detour from the path to avoid meeting a man who carries one. The swearer, standing on stones so that his feet do not touch the ground, strikes the *kithitu* with a stick and swears an oath; he is afterwards ritually cleansed by the owner. It is never used during the rainy season or when the crops are ripening for fear of blighting them, nor should it be used against a relative.

In addition, this oath may be used to seal an agreement or end a feud, or privately in an attempt to harm an enemy. *Kithitu* is thought to kill or vindicate the swearer within six months and, according to Lindblom, he may not have sexual intercourse during that period. A perjurer whose courage fails him may confess and make restitution, after which the owner of the *kithitu* can remove its effects by anointing him with certain ointments.[529]

There is a similar oath called *ndundu* which differs from the *kithitu* chiefly in that its action affects only the swearer and not his family also.

The *kithitu* is taken only by men, there being alternative oaths for women.

Legal Code

Blood-money, that is, the compensation due to the relatives of a murdered man, is the basis on which the amount of damages due for lesser assaults is computed; a man incapacitated by an injury receives full blood-money; if he later dies because of

[527] C. Dundas, 1915, pp. 262, 267.

[528] Lindblom, 1920, p. 154.

[529] Lindblom, 1920, p. 165; Hobley, 1910, p. 168; 1922, p. 239; Dundas, 1915, p. 251; Penwill, 1950, pp. 56–71; Murphy, 2, 1926.

it, his family will receive no more. If he has received a portion and then dies, they receive the rest, no matter how long a time has elapsed.

As the principle is that of compensation rather than punishment, the intention of the offender is immaterial and the same amount is payable whether the injury is due to accident, negligence or intent to cause harm. The actual compensation varies in different districts of Ukamba.[530]

Part of the compensation for homicide is in fact livestock sacrificed at the purification ceremony carried out by the elders. Cattle received as blood-money are never sold or used in marriage payments. Blood-money for women is about half the amount required for men.[531]

Theft, especially of livestock, honey or beehives, is a very serious matter requiring heavy compensation.[532]

Cases for debt are frequent, and mostly arise from marriage transactions. Marriages are legalised by the payment of bridewealth and divorces by its return. The amount is settled by negotiations between the two families. In many marriages the bridewealth is not paid in full until long after the marriage, but until it has been paid the man has not full rights to the wife and children. When it has been paid, the man is the legal husband and the legal father of the woman's children, even though she is living with another man, unless the bridewealth is repaid, and the husband cannot be forced to accept it. The most common grounds for divorce are desertion and barrenness. If the bridewealth is being returned it is necessary to give back the identical animals, even if they have been sold to someone else, and to return every gift made to the woman's father or relatives.[533]

The following analysis of cases tried by one council in 1942 gives an indication of the main causes for which actions are brought:[534]

Blood-money, 5; marriage, 41; land, 73; damage to grazing-land or crops, 87; debt, 289.

Whereas private delicts are settled by arbitration and compensation, with the possibility of a group using self-help if the case is not tried justly, public delicts (especially persistent theft, sorcery or murder) are punished by the judicial process known as *king'oli*. This appears to be similar to the action taken by the Kikuyu *muingi*, described above.[535]

Land Tenure[536]

The use to which land is put and the rights which may be held in it are closely related. The land-holding unit is the joint or extended family (*muvia*), and individual rights in land should be considered within the framework of rights held by the joint family. Land acquired by inheritance used for cultivation is called *ng'undu* and is obtained by demarcating a stretch of land in the commonage (*weu*) which is also used for grazing by any member of the *utui*. A man who does this or acquires rights to cultivate such land by outright purchase from another may dispose of them as he chooses, but on his death they are vested in his joint family. A man who wishes to sell cultivation rights must first offer them to other members of his *mbai* in the same *utui*, and he cannot sell them to an outsider without the permission of the other direct agnatic descendants of the man who first claimed the land. Elders of the *utui* can also control sale indirectly by refusing the right of residence to the purchaser if they consider him or the transaction undesirable. Rights in *ng'undu* are permanent

[530] C. Dundas, 1915, p. 279; Lindblom, 1920, pp. 154 ff. See also Hobley, 1910, p. 79; 1922, pp. 235 ff.; Penwill, 1950, pp. 78–87.

[531] Hobley, 1922, p. 236; Lindblom, 1920, p. 155.

[532] Lindblom, 1920, p. 158; C. Dundas, 1915, p. 275.

[533] C. Dundas, 1915, 285–90; Lindblom, 1920, pp. 73 ff.

[534] Phillips, 1945, p. 102; see also Lindblom, 1920, p. 162.

[535] Lindblom, 1920, pp. 176–82; C. Dundas, 1915, pp. 258, 260; 1913, p. 514; Hobley, 1910, p. 95; 1922, pp. 287–8, Penwill, 1950, pp. 75, 89–92, 196. See above, p. 46.

[536] Lambert, 2, 1947, pp. 142–73; Penwill, 1950, pp. 32–55; Lindblom, 1920, pp. 164–5; C. Dundas, 1921, p. 273; K.L.C. Evidence, II, pp. 1,292 ff.; Liversage, 1945, p. 8.

and in theory a lot never lacks a legitimate "owner"; in practice permanence exists only in the memories of the local inhabitants.

Exclusive grazing rights are established in the *weu* by building and occupying a cattle-post; the land immediately round it is then a grazing area for use of an individual or joint family, and is known as *kisese* (pl, *isese*), as is an uncultivated portion of an *ng'undu* which is being used for grazing. In the case of the former rights of use lapse if not exercised; they can be retained by occupation of the cattle-post, or by frequent visits, by regular renewal of boundary marks or even by proclaiming the intention to return and use the land again. The elders' council of the *utui* can restrict the size of a *kisese* area.

The piece of land worked by a woman in either *ng'undu* or *kisese* land is termed *mbee*. A young wife usually shares the plot of the senior wife and is not allotted her own *mbee* until she has borne children. She will then be shown her first plot and the direction in which she is to work, for each new garden must be above the site of the last in a line parallel with those of her co-wives. A widow retains the right to her *mbee* during her lifetime. Any particularly fertile patch, usually the former site of a homestead or cattle-post, is generally used for sugar-cane or bananas, and gardens may be irrigated.

Beehives are frequently hung in trees in the *weu*, and the owner has certain rights over the ground immediately surrounding the trees: no one who is not a member of the owner's joint family may encroach upon it in any way which might disturb the bees.[537]

Mortgaging of land is common where land is plentiful, but the permission of the co-heirs is needed, as in the case of sale of land-rights, and the elders of the *utui* must consent to the new occupier's residence. Also a man may lend rights in land to a friend. In both cases the tenant-right is heritable, and although in principle the redemption of the land or the eviction of the tenant is possible at any time, the occupier would always be allowed to reap standing crops. A tenant of good character is hardly ever required to leave, and if sale of land becomes necessary he would always be given the chance to buy it. A man may be allotted land-rights by his father-in-law or his brother-in-law, and these rights are heritable, although such tenants have no legal rights over the land and can always be evicted.[538] These three tenant-relationships are closely analogous to the Kikuyu *muguri*, *muhoi* and *muci-arua* or *muthoni*; no other tenant-relationships are mentioned. It would seem that these rights are given only in *ng'undu* land. Land may be given in lieu of livestock for blood-money, but cannot be pledged as security for debts.[539]

Inheritance and Succession

The principle of inheritance is by matri-segmentation; this applies both to land and other possessions. A man divides his land among his wives; on his death they become the nominal heirs and each works her fields until her death, when they pass to her sons.[540] However, Lambert states that the youngest son of a wife stays on the land, the elder sons moving away from their paternal home and founding new homesteads; but the youngest son has no rights in this land as against his brothers, who can come back and claim their shares at any time.[541] If the sons are minors, the next heir acts as trustee: the order of heirs is given as son, father, brother, father's brother. No distinction is made between legitimate and illegitimate children.[542] A woman without sons may "adopt" (although without any adoption ceremony) the son of a co-wife; he may then inherit her chattels and individual

[537] Lambert, 2, 1947, p. 174; Lindblom, 1920, p. 499; Thorp, 1943; Penwill, 1950, pp. 51–3.

[538] Lambert, 2, 1947, pp. 171–4; Hobley, 1910, pp. 83–4; K.L.C. Evidence, II, p. 1, 294; Penwill, 1950, pp. 47–50.

[539] C. Dundas, 1915, p. 267.

[540] Hobley, 1910, p. 83; C. Dundas, 1915, p. 294; 1921, pp. 267, 516; Lindblom, 1920, p. 161; K.L.C. Evidence, II, pp. 1,293–4; Penwill, 1950, pp. 42–7.

[541] Lambert, 2, 1947, p. 146.

[542] C. Dundas, 1915, p. 294; 1921, p. 268; Lindblom, 1920, p. 161.

property. Also a sonless woman can "marry" a wife, as among the Kikuyu: the "wife's" sons will inherit as though born to the woman who "married" her.[543] Livestock in the same way are inherited by the sons of the wife to whose *nza* (kraal) they belong.[544]

Bequests may be made by will, but a man cannot be deprived of his lawful inheritance: that is, apparently, a man can bequeath any particular objects or pieces of land as he likes so long as he does not disregard the principle of inheritance according to matri-segmentation in so doing.[545]

Widows are inherited by the husband's brother, the eldest according to Lindblom, by any brother according to Penwill. Younger wives may be inherited by the sons of other wives; this seems to be a recent development, since formerly it was punished by *king' oli*. There is no evidence to show whether a widow may live as a concubine with another man. All her children belong to her legal husband, i.e. the man who has given bridewealth for her.[546]

MAIN CULTURAL FEATURES

Dress[547]

Traditionally Kamba men went naked or wore only a pubic covering. The proper dress for married women was a calf- or goat-skin rubbed with ochre; women also wore a leather "tail". Girls wore a rectangular skin loin-cloth and an apron made of leather straps threaded with brass wires. Cloth was introduced from the coast during the last century, and the clothing for both sexes then became white or blue cloth, rubbed with fat and ochre, or a blanket. No headgear is worn except that old men may wear a small skull-cap against the sun. Today forms of European clothes are common.

Both sexes, especially women, wear many ornaments, mostly made of wire and beads. Ornaments vary for different age-groups. They consist of belts, collars, necklaces, armlets, leglets, ear- and finger-rings. Necklaces are sometimes made with strongly scented plants.

There are also various coiffures; body hair is removed with tweezers.

The body is perfumed and decorated with ochre. They practise cicatrization and tattooing, and chipping and extraction of teeth. False teeth of hartebeest bone are used to replace teeth decayed as a result of chipping.

Life Cycle

Birth

A pregnant woman does not cohabit with her husband for the last six months of her pregnancy, and during the last three months she must observe certain food prohibitions: she cannot eat fat, honey, beans, or meat of animals killed by poisoned arrows. Lindblom states that pregnant women frequently eat earth from antheaps. They are not regarded as "unclean".[548]

Before the birth, all weapons and iron objects are removed from the hut.[549] There are no special mid-wives, but any women with experience may help at the delivery; the husband may not be present. Hobley states that the woman squats during delivery, Lindblom that she stands. The umbilical cord is cut with a knife,

[543] Lambert, 2, 1947, pp. 166–7.

[544] Penwill, 1950, p. 28.

[545] Lambert, 2, 1947, p. 168; C. Dundas, 1915, p. 296; Hobley, 1910, p. 83; Penwill, 1950, pp. 28–31.

[546] Lindblom, 1920, pp. 78–80, 163; C. Dundas, 1915, pp. 294–5; 1921, p. 267; Hobley, 1910, p. 82; Penwill, 1950, pp. 23–7.

[547] All information as to dress is from Lindblom, 1920, pp. 371–97 and Hobley, 1910, pp. 17–18, 39–42; both accounts are illustrated. See also Larby, 1944, pp. 17–19, and Anon., 1931.

[548] Lindblom, 1920, p. 29; Holbey, 1910, p. 61; Penwill, 1950, states no rules against intercourse during pregnancy.

[549] Hobley, 1922, p. 160.

and the placenta buried outside the hut.[550] One report says that a special door is made in the hut for the mother, and the baby is concealed.[551]

A small boy and girl are sent to fetch water and certain herbs, their behaviour differing according to the sex of the newborn child. The next day one of these children, of the same sex as the baby, carries it to the entrance of the village and back: the mother can then carry her baby on her back.[552]

The father of the child has to fetch four sugar-canes, which are brought to the wife's hut. The third day a feast of meat and beer is held, and the child's name decided.[553] On the fourth day the father hangs an iron necklace on the child's neck; this done, the child is regarded as a human being and loses contact with the spirit world. Before this a child is called *kiimu* (cf. *aimu*, ancestor spirit), and should such a child die its mother is ritually unclean. That night the parents have ritual intercourse, and the baby is placed between the woman's breasts, the place in which it sleeps until her next menstruation. If the mother is unmarried, this intercourse is carried out by a "friend" of the girl's father. At the next menstruation the parents have ritual intercourse again, and the baby is placed behind its mother's back.[554]

The mother stays in the hut with the child for twenty days, according to Hobley, but Lindblom says she may well return to normal life even on the day of birth, if she wishes.[555]

A child born feet first or in a caul may only marry another person born in the same manner. The birth of twins brings misfortune, and it seems that formerly one was killed or the mother was sent back to her father and the bridewealth returned. A child who cuts the upper teeth first is also subject to certain prohibitions.[556]

INITIATION[557]

To become a fully adult member of the tribe a man or woman must undergo two initiation ceremonies: *nzaiko ila nini* (the small circumcision) and *nzaiko ila nene* (the great circumcision), the second of which is regarded as the more important. There is a third ceremony for men only called *nzaiko ya aume* (the circumcision of the men) or *mbavani*. There are various alternative names for these rites. They are held in this order during the longer dry season, August to October, the first two yearly and the third only every few years. It seems that the third rite may only take place in eastern Kamba.

The essential element of the first ceremony is circumcision or clitoridectomy; the age of the initiates may be as low as four or five years, since the rite has no connection with puberty, but depends rather on the ability of the child's father to pay the fees of the operators. An elder who wishes his son to be circumcised arranges for the ceremony to take place and all the children of the *utui* or *kibali* who are ready for initiation assemble at his homestead.

The operator and his wife, who usually operates upon the girls (removing the prepuce of the clitoris and the *labia minora*), are specialists. The ceremony is accompanied by public dances, beer drinks for the fathers of the circumcised children and sacrifices to the ancestors.

The candidates for the second or great *nzaiko* are generally between eight and twelve years old. The same operator and his wife may officiate in the first part of the ceremony, during which both boys and girls live together in a specially erected large hut in the *thome*, where they receive ritual and practical instruction from instructors. They learn special songs and encounter symbolic obstacles on the first day; on the second the boys must prove their courage by confronting a ritual monster

[550] Hobley, 1910, p. 50; Lindblom, 1920, p. 31.
[551] Lindblom, 1920, p. 32.
[552] Lindblom, 1920, p. 33.
[553] Lindblom, 1920, p. 33; Hobley, 1910, p. 60; Penwill, 1950, p. 8.
[554] Lindblom, 1920, pp. 34–5; Hobley, 1910, p. 60; Penwill, 1950, p. 9.
[555] Hobley, 1910, p. 61; Lindblom, 1920, p. 31.
[556] Lindblom, 1920, pp. 37–8; Hobley, 1910, p. 61; 1922, p. 157; Penwill (1950, p. 14) states twins were not killed.
[557] Lindblom, 1920, pp. 42–68; Hobley, 1910, pp. 67–77; Larby, 1944, pp. 12–13.

called *mbusya* (buffalo)—in reality a structure of sticks and branches which emits frightening bellows—while the girls have a similar terrifying ordeal. Their nights in the hut are spent in singing obscene songs and in bawdy conversation, but sexual intercourse is forbidden. The operator and his wife must, however, have ritual coitus on the night before the ceremony begins and on the second night after, and the parents of the candidates on the third night and the seventh.

On the third morning the operator, his wife, and the instructors receive their fees, after which the candidates engage symbolically upon the tasks of adults. The boys are sent hunting with miniature bows, while the girls "break twigs", a token of the woman's job of collecting firewood. Before returning home they are blessed by the operator and his wife who spit beer over them.

At home they are required to discover the meaning or peculiarities of various objects laid out or to guess what actions they must perform. During the dances called *nzuma*, which are held during the second part of the ceremony and in which only the circumcised may take part, the boys make mock sexual assaults upon the girls with a special short stick that each has been given. On the fourth day the candidates are questioned as to the meaning of certain "pictographic riddles" (Hobley) which are carved on sticks or drawn in sand; they must also steal sugar-cane to make beer for the instructors.

On the fifth day the instructors hold a ceremony at a sacred fig-tree, each taking a little of the milky juice from its trunk, which is given to the novices who pretend to eat it; after this they are allowed certain foods which were forbidden during the preceding days. At the fig-tree also the boys undergo a second operation, a slight cut being made at the base of the *glans penis* and beer poured into it. There are no particular observances on the sixth day. On the seventh the boys carry out a mock cattle raid; in Kikumbuliu they must steal the yellow fruit of *solanum* which is guarded by cowherds, and in Ulu they attack the herds as they are being driven home in the evening, using the same fruit as missiles, while the women cry out that the Masai have come. This concludes the ceremonies.

The participants in the third *nzaiko*, the "circumcision of the men", are bound by an oath of secrecy; Lindblom speaks of the great difficulty of getting any information on the subject[558] and Hobley in fact learned very little of the true nature of the rites.[559] They take place far away from the homesteads and the participants live in a special hut built near a river by men who have already undergone this ceremony. These men also build a *mbavani*, which is the equivalent of the *mbusya* used in the second *nzaiko*. They carry it at night to the operator's village. Songs are sung and the candidates are led to the selected place, without having seen the *mbavani*; with them go the operators whose role is that of protectors, particularly from the group of younger men, whose function it is to torment the initiates. Each group sits by its own fire for a feast, the meat for which is provided by the candidates as fees. They are then blindfolded and in a sandy place *mbavani* is again produced. Tests of endurance and sexual prowess are performed during the next two days; during this time the candidates are plagued and hampered by their tormentors, whom they must treat with exaggerated deference and respect, while submitting to indignities such as being forced to eat their fæces. They are given no food and at the end of the tests are allowed to sleep in their homes; on the following five or six days there are great dances. At first the candidates, who have again left their homes, are not regarded as human beings responsible for their actions, and they may attack with impunity anyone who crosses their path. If anyone is killed, not the candidate but his instructor is considered guilty. The only people who escape assault are those men who have themselves been through the third *nzaiko*, which fact they establish by the knowledge of secret signs. After a few days the candidates return home, where they may not speak to their parents until they have slept, washed and dressed, and a little hair has been shaved from the foreheads. They are then regarded as full social beings again and the ceremonies are over.

[558] Lindblom, 1920, p. 60.
[559] Hobley, 1911, p. 75.

It is customary also for young men to have their teeth chipped, the incisors being cut to points. Hobley says that this forms part of the first *nzaiko*, but Lindblom considers that it is merely a tribal fashion, intended to beautify, and not obligatory. According to Dundas, different styles are characteristic of the different districts of Ukamba.[560]

Betrothal and Marriage[561]

Pre-marital intercourse is permitted among the Kamba, but it is shameful for an unmarried girl to become pregnant. Abortion is practised.[562] Girls are married between 12 and 18 years of age, men later. The Kamba are polygynous.

There is an elaborate sequence of gifts of goats and beer made by the suitor to the father of the girl, leading up to negotiations as to the amount of bridewealth, which consists of cattle and goats; transfer of bridewealth may be spread out over many years. In addition, a suitor must give preliminary gifts to the girl's mother and other close kin, and he also works in her father's fields.

The bride is fetched by her husband and taken to his home in the evening, quietly, where she is welcomed by his mother who smears her neck with fat. Symbolic abduction is not usual among the Kamba, as it is among the Kikuyu, although Lindblom mentions a case. The groom, when he goes to fetch the bride, takes gifts for her mother and a bullock, which is cut into two, the mother being given one half and he and his "friends" the other. The couple sleep together but without intercourse on the first night. Next day (Lindblom) or two days later (Penwill) the girls of her group visit her and wail and are given presents. The bride is then considered a married woman.

The husband makes further gifts to his affines. The new wife must observe certain avoidances towards her affines. The couple usually live in the husband's mother's hut until the birth of the first child.

A man normally defers to his first wife's wishes as to his second wife.[563]

Divorce is said to be uncommon; grounds for a husband sending his wife back to her father include lack of industry, unfaithfulness or witchcraft on her part. A wife's barrenness is not a reason for divorce, but sterility or cruelty on the part of a man gives his wife a reason for leaving him. Sterility is not a common reason since a woman may have intercourse with the half-brother corresponding to her husband in seniority within each "house". The bridewealth is not usually returned until the wife has remarried (progeny of the original cattle must be returned, but only the original number of goats); but a husband may refuse to accept the bridewealth, in which case her future children are his.[564]

The Kamba practise "ghost" marriage: a girl is married to the name of an unmarried man who has died. She bears him children, usually by his brother as genitor.[565]

Death and Burial[566]

The disposal of corpses differs from one area to another, since the method is changed if an unusually large number of deaths occur in one area in a short time. A dying man is watched by elders; only they may touch a corpse. In the less crowded areas, especially in the east, only elders and first wives are buried, other corpses being thrown into the bush. But in the west and in crowded areas all dead bodies are buried. The grave is round and about a yard deep. The body is laid on its side, hunched up, a man on his right side and a woman on her left, both with

[560] Hobley, 1910, p. 18; Lindblom, 1920, pp. 70, 392; C. Dundas, 1913, p. 498; 1915, p. 240.
[561] Lindblom, 1920, pp. 72–82, 89–98; Hobley, 2, 1910, pp. 62–5; Penwill, 1950, pp. 1–7.
[562] Lindblom, 1920, pp. 38–9.
[563] Penwill, 1950, pp. 9–10.
[564] Lindblom, 1920, pp. 82–4; Larby, 1944, p. 14; Penwill, 1950, pp. 10–20.
[565] Hobley, 1922, pp. 30–1; C. Dundas, 1915, pp. 287–8.
[566] Lindblom, 1920, pp. 103–10; Hobley, 1910, pp. 66–7; 1922, pp. 101–2; Larby, 1944, p. 15.

the head resting on the hand, man facing east, woman west. The body is naked but for a cloth or blanket over the face to keep earth off it; in Ulu no personal possessions are placed in the grave except that a woman is buried in her personal ornaments, but in the east certain possessions are placed with the corpse. An elder is buried outside his hut, which continues to be used; a married woman is buried in the cattle kraal if her husband has no hut except hers; if he has another she is buried in her hut, which is shut up without her chattels being disturbed and allowed to fall down. A childless junior wife is taken through a specially made opening in the village fence and placed in the bush. A man's grave is dug by the elders, the first sod being turned by his son's son with a grave-stick; for this he is given a beast by his father's sister. Stones are placed over the grave, and the place is not disturbed. Children are buried by old women, not by male elders: a child so young that its two lower incisors have not been removed has them knocked out after death. A man mortally sick is sometimes exposed in the bush.

The women of a village mourn for two to five days and do no field work. The village is ritually unclean and is purified on the third day: an elder of *makwa*[567] slaughters a goat and sprinkles the feet and legs of the members with the contents of its stomach. The deceased's parents perform ritual intercourse, as do the widows with his successor. Until this is done, the members of the village may not have intercourse, nor may other kin visit them.

Religious Beliefs and Ritual

The religion of the Kamba consists of a well-developed ancestral cult and a vague conception of a higher power. This higher power is called *Ngai*, *Mulungu* or *Mumbi* (the creator). It is not personified and is such an amorphous being that it has been suggested that the terms *Ngai* or *Mulungu* may denote simply the supernatural, including the ancestor spirits. Dundas says that the terms are interchangeable.[568] *Ngai* is the word used by the Masai for a supreme deity and where Kamba borders Masai in the south-west a sharper distinction is drawn between *Ngai* and the ancestor spirits.[569] *Ngai* is in the sky and is held to be well-disposed towards mankind but to have little to do with them; the Kamba pay little attention to him in the way of sacrifice. Prayers, especially for rain, are sometimes addressed to *Ngai*.[570]

The *aimu* (sing. *imu*) are the spirits of the dead, both men and women;[571] the *imu*, which during life is known as *kiu* (soul or shadow) or *ngoo* (life), leaves the body at death; its departure, in fact, constitutes death. The world of the spirits is not always localized, but in Southern Kitui and Kibwezi it is believed to be on Mount Kyumbe (at the southern end of the Chyulu range), which is never called by its name but is referred to as *Mulungu* or *Ngai*[572] (although the names of the dead themselves are not avoided).[573] There the *aimu* live much the same sort of life as they did while still alive.[574] The souls of sorcerers are said to be banished to waste places.[575] *Aimu* generally live in trees, preferably fig-trees of the species *muumo* or *muumbu*, or in other prominent natural features, solitary rocks or pools, which are therefore places of sacrifice.[576] They live on the food which is offered to them in sacrifices, and require constant attention; the least dereliction of duty on the part of their descendants is punished by misfortune in the shape of accidents and disease to men

[567] A ritual elder, see below, p. 86.

[568] Lindblom, 1920, pp. 209, 243, 247; Hobley, 1910, p. 85; C. Dundas, 1913, p. 535; Lambert, 2, 1947, p. 134.

[569] Lindblom, 1920, p. 247.

[570] Lindblom, 1920, pp. 46, 244–5; Lambert, 2, 1947, p. 134.

[571] Lindblom, 1920, p. 307; C. Dundas, 1913, p. 535; Hobley, 1922, p. 27; Lambert, 2, 1947, p. 134; Nottingham, 1959, pp. 7–8. Hobley (1910, p. 85) suggests that certain important people may have more than one *imu*.

[572] Lindblom, 1920, p. 210.

[573] Lindblom, 1920, p. 215.

[574] Lindblom, 1920, pp. 209 ff.; C. Dundas, 1913, p. 535.

[575] Hobley, 1910, p. 89.

[576] Lindblom, 1920, pp. 219, 288; C. Dundas, 1913, p. 537; Hobley, 1910, p. 85; 1922, p. 28.

and herds. A man goes to a diviner to enquire the causes of misfortune. Malevolen *aimu* can, however, sometimes be duped.[577] If the ancestors are pleased they will sen good fortune or warnings of impending epidemics or raids, speaking in dreams to th *mundu mue* (medicine man) or through a medium.[578] The *aimu* appear most frequentl in dreams but sometimes they assume a material non-human form to visit the living If any normally timid animal, like a wild cat, fearlessly approaches a homestead, it i thought to be harbouring an *imu* and food may be thrown to it; snakes, particularl pythons, are also thought to be favourite vehicles. Occasionally the *aimu* take near human form and there are legends of unusually tall one-legged men who sto travellers on lonely roads.[579] The *aimu* are said to appear less frequently since th arrival of the Europeans. Sometimes, although remaining invisible, they can be hear calling and beating their drums.[580] Nottingham mentions the figures of Mupite, a mal spirit associated with the *aimu* of Kanta who have died away from home and becom lost to their descendants, and Kathambi, a female spirit dwelling in valleys an streams. Sacrifices are made to them and they are also used by witches.[581]

Every woman has a spirit husband as well as her human one, and he is though to be largely responsible for her fertility, for the Kamba believe that although sexua intercourse is necessary for conception it is not by itself sufficient. A woman is liabl to be possessed by this spirit, who, speaking through her, may announce his name. I she does not become pregnant within six months or so of marriage sacrifice is offere to her spirit husband.[582]

Some births, though not all, are held to be reincarnations of ancestors, eithe because the ancestor has appeared in a dream to the pregnant woman and announce his impending rebirth, or because he is recognized in the child by the presence o some birthmark, deformity or other characteristic. Such a child is named after th ancestor even though he is not necessarily of the same sex.[583] The ancestors giv information to the medicine men about the herbs and objects to be used in ritua and to cure diseases.[584]

The offering of food is the essential element of most Kamba rituals and is calle *kithanguna*, the word also used for magical medicines, both the harmless varieti (such as love potions) and the malevolent intended to kill.[585]

Sacrifices may be offered to the *aimu* in the hut—a little food and drink fro each meal being placed upon the floor—or at the shrines called *ithembo* (pl. *mathemb* with a request for a particular benefit or protection. According to Hobley prayers fo rain, at least, are offered to *Ngai* and he distinguishes two kinds of shrines, on dedicated to the *aimu* and one to *Ngai*; both are called *ithembo*, and the sacrifice are made in the same way by the *atumia ma ithembo* and the *iveti sya ithembo*, the female counterparts.[586] Lambert also speaks of two sorts of shrine, the *ithembo* servin a *kivalo* and the *kitunyeo kya ng'ondu* serving an *utui*.[587] *Ng'ondu* is the act of purifi cation in which various purifying liquids are used in magical and religious rituals; the principal ingredients are parts of special plants and sometimes certain of the intestine or stomach contents of an animal, generally a goat.[588] The term *kitunyeo*, on the oth hand, is not mentioned by any other authority and Stanner says that he never hear of any word other than *ithembo* for a place of sacrifice.[589] Lambert's statements abo

[577] Lindblom, 1920, pp. 215–16; C. Dundas, 1913, pp. 535–6.
[578] Lindblom, 1920, pp. 212, 227; Hobley, 1910, p. 85; 1922, p. 59, says that the messages are sent by *Ngai*.
[579] Lindblom, 1920, pp. 26, 212–13; Hobley, 1910, pp. 86 ff.; 1922, p. 30; C. Dunda 1913, p. 535.
[580] Lindblom, 1920, p. 216.
[581] Nottingham, 1959, p. 7–8.
[582] Hobley, 1910, p. 89; Lindblom, 1920, p. 211.
[583] Lindblom, 1920, pp. 36, 212; Hobley, 1910, p. 39; 1922, p. 157.
[584] Lindblom, 1920, p. 255.
[585] Lindblom, 1920, pp. 218, 281.
[586] Hobley, 1922, p. 53; Penwill, 1950, pp. 113–14.
[587] Lambert, 2, 1947, p. 134.
[588] Lambert, 2, 1947, p. 134.
[589] Stanner, personal communication.

he *kitunyeo* have therefore been treated as referring to the *ithembo*.

Mathembo are very numerous, particularly around Machakos, where they are ometimes only a few minutes' walk apart; presumably they vary in importance, ne being used for rites on behalf of a whole *utui* and others only for a single family roup.[590] Sacrifices on behalf of the joint family are made by the family head, for a nan may not sacrifice while his father is living and a woman may only do so when pecially instructed by a *mundu mue*. Such sacrifices are made at family crises such s a birth, or when they are thought necessary to placate the ancestors after a run of nisfortune or sickness, but never during certain months. Arms may not be taken into n *ithembo*, nor may anything be killed there, and it is regarded as a sanctuary; ccording to Hobley, this immunity extends to the person of a ritual elder.[591]

An *ithembo* is generally a grove with one or two large trees, preferably fig-trees r, where these are scarce, as in Kitui, baobab; there may also be a rock or some atural feature supposed to be frequented by an *imu*, sometimes a miniature hut on r beside his grave. Such huts are also built at the foot of the trees and offerings laced in them. The sacrificial animal is generally a goat, sometimes a bullock or a ull, a sheep or a fowl if the *mundu mue* advises it; but whatever the animal it must e of one colour, never spotted or piebald, and without blemish or deformity. In ertain ceremonies designed to increase the crops the hyrax or its dung may be used. n the case of a public sacrifice, offered on behalf of the *utui*, the victim is provided y each *mutamia ma ithembo*, of which there are generally about ten or twelve, in urn.

The *mundu mue* decides when a particular rite shall be performed and what orm it shall take, but however high his rank as an elder he may take no further art, neither presenting the sacrificial animal nor cutting the meat.

All sacrificial ceremonies are carried out in much the same way, but there is no ixed order of ritual or prayer which can be nullified by a mistake. Public sacrifices re made for rain, at the planting time, when a portion of a crop is gathered before t is ripe, when the first fruits are harvested, in Kibwezi at threshing time, on eturning from a successful raid, when the first ox is killed, and to purify the village fter an epidemic.[592]

Descriptions of sacrifices at the *ithembo* are given by Lindblom and Hobley.[593] Both male and female elders of the ritual grade enter the *ithembo*; they are attended y the other members of the group, who, however, may not enter the grove. The fferings are made by the elders, the sacrificial meat being shared by everyone resent. The elders abstain from sexual intercourse for one day before and six days fter the ceremony.

Several authorities record what was already a tradition to the Kamba, that vhen drought was prolonged and all the usual ceremonies had produced no result, child, possibly a Kikuyu captive but failing that a Kamba child, was buried alive n an *ithembo*. According to Lindblom such a child was taken from the Ambua rain) clan or the Aei clan in Kitui, but Lambert says that it was the Ambua or Anziu lan; its family received token compensation. Large areas, comprising several *ivalo*, vould unite for such a ceremony.[594]

There are no rain-making techniques other than sacrifices to the ancestors or *Ngai*, and the avoidance of any acts which will prevent rain. The use of iron implenents and in fact any unusual occurrence is thought to cause drought: the building of he railway was held responsible for several bad years.[595]

[590] Lindblom, 1920, p. 219.

[591] Hobley, 1922, p. 64.

[592] Hobley, 1922, pp. 5, 60–1, 76; Lindblom, 1920, pp. 220, 223, 257; C. Dundas, 1913, . 527.

[593] Lindblom, 1920, pp. 221–3, 275–6; Hobley, 1922, pp. 53–6, 60; also Beresford-Stooke, , 1928.

[594] Lindblom, 1920, p. 224; Lambert, 2, 1947, p. 136; Hobley, 1910, p. 57.

[595] Lindblom, 1920, p. 224; C. Dundas, 1913, p. 500.

RITUAL UNCLEANNESS

The state of *makwa* which, if not removed, results in sores, wasting and eventually death, is a supernatural sanction enforcing rules of conduct. The actions which cause it are, for the most part, the disregarding of the rules of purification, particularly after a death, and the anticipation of inheritance, whether it be of a man's father's beehives or his widows. A list of actions which bring *thavu* and *makwa* is given by Hobley.[596] A man who commits adultery with a married woman while the cattle are out grazing runs the risk of infection and the mother of a baby who dies must have her breasts purified before she can suckle another. It is also the punishment of a man who kills or eats his totem.

Makwa or *thavu* is removed by various rituals, some sacrificial, but all including the use of purificatory liquid.[597] A special class of ritual officers, the *atumia ma makwa* are qualified to remove ritual uncleanness.[598] Hobley states that a man can become a *mutamia ma makwa* if his wife has "died in circumstances which might afflict him with *makwa*", but does not explain further. If he is treated successfully, he is considered to have been initiated and, after gaining experience, achieves the position of a specialist. Lindblom distinguishes between *thavu*, which he equates with the Kikuyu *thahu*, and *makwa* which he calls a more serious condition. The former is dealt with by *atumia ukuu*, the latter by *atumia ma makwa.*[599]

It seems clear that the concept or concepts of *makwa-thavu* are very similar to the Kikuyu *thahu*, but far less important, fewer actions and situations being considered dangerous; the Kamba are said to despise the Kikuyu for being "*makwa* ridden".[600]

There is a class of purificatory rituals of which the most important is purification after a homicide. It is directed by a special class of elder, the *atumia ma ukuu*. Their function is to ward off death, and the necessary qualification is a series of deaths among the elders' close kin during a short period. The purification protects the families of both murderer and murdered man from further calamity.[601] The weapon with which a man has been killed is dangerous in itself and is got rid of by being given to a passer-by or left on a path.[602]

A dying person can put a curse (*kiume*) on his close agnatic and matrilineal kin. Hobley describes it as "*thabu* or *makwa* which can be suspended by a dying man over his descendants". Such a curse usually refers to the offering of hospitality to the dying man's friends, the alienation of a piece of land, and so on. The curse can be lifted by an elder related to the dead man. It is analogous to the Kikuyu *kirume.*[603]

MAGIC AND SORCERY

There are two kinds of magical practitioner, as among the Kikuyu, the *mundu mue* (pl. *aue*) or medicine man, whose work is beneficial, and the *mundu mwoi*, a sorcerer.[604]

A man, or, more rarely, a woman, becomes *mundu mue* because he is chosen by the ancestor spirits. His future may be apparent at birth (such a child is born with some appendage or perhaps a small peg clasped in his fist) or a child of normal birth may have a solitary disposition and have dreams of the ancestors. All knowledge of magical materials and techniques is derived from this source. *Mundu aue* are either

[596] Hobley, 1922, pp. 128–34.
[597] Lindblom, 1920, pp. 296, 324.
[598] Hobley, 1911, pp. 413–14; 1922, pp. 127–31.
[599] Lindblom, 1922, pp. 298–301.
[600] Hobley, 1922, p. 127; Lindblom, 1920, p. 300; Nottingham, 1959, pp. 9–10.
[601] C. Dundas, 1913, p. 513; 1915, p. 270; 1921, p. 243; Lindblom, 1920, p. 155; Hobley, 1911, pp. 414, 426; 1922, pp. 223–4, 235.
[602] Hobley, 1911, p. 427; 1922, p. 237; C. Dundas, 1915, p. 270.
[603] Hobley, 1922, pp. 145, 152–3; 1, 1911, p. 431.
[604] Lindblom, 1920, pp. 173–5, 254–85, 465, 537; C. Dundas, 1913, pp. 528–34; Hobley, 1910, p. 89; Penwill, 1950, pp. 93–6; Nottingham, 1959, pp. 4–5.

diviners or healers, seldom both. A successful man may gain a great reputation and fame. They increase their prestige with conjuring tricks and by claiming to perform miracles.[605]

There are two main divining techniques: interpretation of the diviner's own dreams, and the use of a divining calabash. The diviner gets into touch with the ancestors by means of a drumming bow[606] and interprets the positions of various objects thrown from the calabash.[607] Details of belief regarding techniques and poisons used by the sorcerer are given by Nottingham.[608] The power is transmitted from a woman to her daughter, on pain of *thavu*; it may also be given to any female affine.

The *mundu mue* prescribes amulets, made by weavers to his specifications; they contain medicines or have magical designs.[609] He knows the secret rites which will confer efficacy on medicines, the composition of which may be publicly known.[610] He can prophesy future disasters, administer legal ordeals and detect sorcerers. *Mundu aue* who are healers rather than diviners are also called *itima*; diseases come from the ancestors, sorcery or "natural causes" and a different type of specialist must be consulted for each different type of disease.[611]

The *mundu mue* has considerable prestige but no specific influence outside his professional field; it seems that in many ways he is regarded as having feminine characteristics. After his burial the elders sacrifice and dance at his grave; he himself, like women and children, may never touch a corpse. His divinatory and magical apparatus are not inherited but remain until his spirit appears to someone and gives instructions for their disposal.[612]

Spirit Possession

States of dissociation and certain kinds of hysterical fit occur frequently among the Kamba, especially among women, and are regarded as possession by a spirit. The ancestor spirits are thought to speak through a medium and possession by them is not feared. It commonly occurs at dances, and the spirit is exorcised by dancing. The type of possession, its effects and the form of the exorcism rite may vary from year to year. Hobley calls the phenomenon "infectious mania", and there are good descriptions of the *Kijesu* dances of 1906 and of the Kitombo and Kisuka. The possessed slashed themselves with knives, walked on fire, and spoke with tongues. Individual possession seems to have been precipitated by the sight of a European or of European clothing.[613] The *ngai* mania of 1911 was more complex and was suppressed by the Government.[614]

[605] Lindblom, 1920, pp. 265–8; C. Dundas, 1913, p. 528.

[606] Lindblom, 1920, pp. 258–9; 402–3 (illus.).

[607] C. Dundas, 1913, p. 531; Beresford-Stooke, 4, 1928.

[608] Nottingham, 1959, *passim*.

[689] Lindblom, 1920, pp. 241, 285–8, 442, 466; Hobley, 1912.

[610] Lindblom, 1920, pp. 270–1; C. Dundas, 1913, p. 529; Beresford-Stooke, 3, 1928; details of the cleansing of sorcerers are given by Nottingham, 1959, p. 11–12.

[611] Lindblom, 1920, pp. 257–8; C. Dundas, 1913, pp. 529–30.

[612] Lindblom, 1920, pp. 257–8; C. Dundas, 1913, p. 530.

[613] C. Dundas, 1913, p. 536; Hobley, 1910, pp. 85–6; 1922, pp. 30, 255; Lindblom, 1920, pp. 229–31; Neligan, 1911, p. 49.

[614] Murphy, 1926, pp. 200–6; Hobley, 1922, pp. 255–8; in this context, *ngai* does not refer to God.

BIBLIOGRAPHY

There are many early travellers' works which contain passing references to Kikuyu and Kamba; these are not given here, nor are the references given by Schapera to files in the Secretariat, Nairobi, which are not publicly available in this country. Names of authors of evidence to the Kenya Land Commission, 1932, which are given separately by Schapera, are omitted. Reference on the text is always to the page of the printed evidence only.

Anderson, T. F. Kikuyu diet. E. Afr. med. J., *14*, 1937, 120–31.

Arkell-Hardwick, A. An ivory trader in north Kenia. London. 1903.
Northern tribes. A poor account, but containing a good description of the country. Contains names of many "sections" and clans.

Armstrong, R. G. East Africa. Phylon, *16*, 4, 1955, 435–47.

Askwith, T. Medicine for Mau Mau. Corona, *8*, 1, Jan. 1956, 5–8.

Augustiny, J. Tribes of Ukamba: their history, customs, etc. E. Afr. quart., 2, 1905, 405–13.
——Erlebnisse eines Kambajungen von ihm selbst erzählt. Z. Eingeb.-Spr., 10, 1920, 161–80.
——Kambamärchen. Z. Eingeb.-Spr., 15, 1924–5, 81–116, 213–23.

Baker, R. S. B. Kabongo: the story of a Kikuyu chief. Oxford: G. Ronald. 1955.

Barlow, A. R. The *mugumo* tree in connection with Kikuyu circumcision ceremonies. J. E. Afr. Uganda nat hist. Soc., *3*, 6, July, 1913, 41–44.
A good description of the "Great dance".
Kikuyu land-tenure and heritance. J. E. Afr. nat. His. Soc., nos. 45–6, Apr.–July, 1932, 56–66.
Valuable for its factual material.

Barra, G. 1000 Kikuyu proverbs. London: Macmillan. 1960.

Barrett, W. E. H. A Kikuyu fairy tale. Man, *12*, 22, 1912, 41–42; 57, 112–13; 98, 183–5; *13*, 6, 1913, 10–11; 14, 14–25; 44, 73–76.
Translation of fairy tales.

Barton, G. A. Sacrifice among the Wakamba. J. Amer. folklore, *12*, 1899, 144–5.

Beech, M. W. H. The sacred fig-tree of the A-Kikuyu of East Africa. Man, *13*, 3, 1913, 4–6. [Referred to in footnotes as 1, 1913.]
——Suicide amongst the Kikuyu of East Africa. Man, *13*, 30, 1913, 56–57.
A short account of suicide case.
——A ceremony at a *mugumu* or sacred fig-tree of the A-Kikuyu of East Africa. Man, *13*, 51, 1913, 86–89.
Description of purifying a newly built dam.
——Pre-Bantu occupants of East Africa. Man, *15*, 24, 1915, 40–41.
Short account of the Agumba.
——Kikuyu system of land tenure. J. Afr. Soc., *17*, 65, Oct. 1917, 46–59; *17*, 66, Jan. 1918, 136–44.
Kikuyu, Northern tribes. Contains much valuable factual material.

Beecher, L. J. The African explains witchcraft. 3. Kikuyu. Africa, *8*, 4, Oct. 1935, 516–19.
——The stories of the Kikuyu, Africa, *11*, 1, 1938, 80–81.
Of little value.
——The Kikuyu. Nairobi: C.M.S. Press. 1944.
Short general account; inadequate, but has useful description of the "guilds".

Beidelman, T. O. Some notes on the Kamba of Kilosa District. Tanganyika notes, 57, Sept. 1961, 181–94.

Beresford-Stooke, G. An Akamba ceremony used in times of draught. Man, *28*, 105, 1928, 193-40.
Rain-making offering by women. [Referred to in footnotes as 1, 1928.]
——Akamba ceremonies connected with dreams. Man, *28*, 128, 1928, 176–7.
Article on good and bad dreams. [Referred to in footnotes as 2, 1928.]
——Ceremonies designed to influence the fertility of women. Man, *28*, 129, 928, p. 177.
Kamba. Description of magic medicine. [Referred to in footnotes as 3, 1928.]
——An Akamba fortune-telling ceremony. Man, *28*, 137, 1928, p. 189.
Divination by throwing seeds. [Referred to in footnotes as 4, 1928.]

Bernardi, B. The Mugwe, a failing prophet: a study of a religious and public dignitary of the Meru of Kenya. London: Oxford Univ. Press for Int. Afr. Inst. 1959.

Bewes, T. F. C. Kikuyu religion—old and new. Afr. affairs, *52*, 208, July 1953, 202–10.

Blackwood, M. J. H. Kitui Kamba. J. roy. anthrop. Inst., 56, 1926, 195–206.

Boninger, J. New ways of living for the Kamba tribesmen. Community development Bull., *7*, 2, 1956, 28–30.

Bordoni, L. Un pueblo salvaje y feliz; los Kikuyu. Rev. geog. americana, 1, 1933, 181–7.

Boyes J. King of the Kikuyu. London. 1911.
Boyes reached Kikuyu in 1898 and was the first European in west Kikuyu: he lived there for two years. The book, though often unreliable, gives some valuable data.

Braunholtz, H. J. A peculiar type of armlet. Man, *21*, 37, 1921, 65–67.

Brom, J. L. Mau-Mau. Paris: Amiot-Dumont. 1956.

Brutzer, E. Begegnungen mit Wakamba. Leipzig. 1902.
——Was kamba Jungen treiben. Leipzig. 1905.
——Der Geisterglaube bei den Kamba. Leipzig. 1905.
——Tierfabeln der Kamba. Arch. f. Anthrop., 37, 1910, 23–42.

Bugeau, F. La circoncision au Kikuyu. Anthropos, *6*, 1911, 616–27.
Contains good account of circumcision ceremony.
——Les Wakikouyous et la guerre. Ann. lateranensi, *7*, 1943, 183–226.
Full account of Kikuyu warfare and war organization.

Bunche, R. J. The land question in Kenya as seen by a Kikuyu chief. J. Negro Hist., 24, 1939, 33–35.
——The Irua ceremony among the Kikuyu of Kiambu. J. Negro Hist., 26, 1941, 46–55.

Cagnolo, C. The Akikuyu: their customs, traditions and folklore. Nyeri: Mission Printing School. 1933.
Written by a Catholic missionary of the Consolata Fathers. The book is useful, on the purely descriptive level. Much of it deals with effects of Christianity in Kikuyu. Sections on arts, beliefs, etc., are in great detail. Many illustrations.
——Gli Aghekoio. Turin: Consolata Mission. 1940–1944.
——Kikuyu tales. Afr. studies, *11*, 1, Mar. 1952, 1–15; 3, Sept., 122–35; *12*, 1, Mar. 1953, 10–21; 3, Sept. 122–31.

Carothers, J. C. The psychology of Mau Mau. Nairobi: Govt. Printer. 1954.

Cayzac, P. La religion des Kikuyu. Anthropos, *5*, 1910, 309–19.
Good article on *ngai* ancestor cult and circumcision.
——Witchcraft in Kikuyu. Man, *12*, 67, 1912, p. 127.
Short article on magicians' tricks.

Chambers, P. C. Native methods of food storage. E. Afr. agric. J., 55, 1939, 99–103.
Embu, Meru, Kamba.

Champion, A. M. The Atharaka. J. roy. anthrop. Inst., *42*, 1912, 68–90.
A useful article, dealing mostly with material culture. Apart from articles by C. Dundas, is the only account of this tribe.

Cloete, S. Storm over Africa: a study of the Mau Mau rebellion. Cape Town: Culemborg. 1956.

Colpi, E. Credenze religiose e moralità Kikuyu. Turin: Ed. Filosofia. 1953.

Corfield, F. D. Historical survey of the origins and growth of Mau Mau. London: H.M.S.O. 1960.

Crawford, J. W. W. The Kikuyu medicine man. Man, *9*, 30, 1909, 53–56.
Brief account of activities of *mundu mugo*.

Crawshay, R. Kikuyu: notes on the country, people, fauna and flora. Geog. J., *20*, 1902, 24–49.
A good and detailed account; has little on social organization.

Danby, P. M. A study of the physique of some native East Africans (mainly Kikuyu). J. roy. anthrop. Inst., *83*, 2, July-Dec. 1953, 194–214.

de Monfried, H. Sous le masque Mau-Mau. Paris: Grasset. 1956.

de Pree, H. Notes of a journey on the Tana river, 1879. Geog. J., 17, 1901, 512–16.

de Roock, J. D. Achtergronden van de Mau-Mau beweging in Kenya. Int. spectator, *9*, 17, 8 Sept. 1955, 594–610.

Dessy, G. B. Considerazioni sul fenomeno Mau Mau. Affrica, *10*, 3, Mar. 1955, 86–87.

Dickson, B. The eastern borderlands of Kikuyu. Geog. J., *21*, 1903, 36–39.
Of little value; mentions a few place-names.

Doke, C. M. Bantu: modern grammatical, phonetical, and lexicographical studies since 1860. London: Percy Lund, Humphries for Int. Afr. Inst. 1945.
Contains short account of the place of Kikuyu and Kamba in the Bantu languages.

Dougall, J. W. C., *and* Itotia, J. The voice of Africa: Kikuyu proverbs. Africa, *1*, 4, Oct. 1928, 486–90.

Dundas, C. History of Kitui. J. roy, anthrop. Inst., *43*, 1913, 480–549.
Kamba, Tharaka. Dundas was a Government Officer. This is a straightforward account of the Kitui Kamba with some notes on Tharaka. Not as good as his later articles but far above the average material on these peoples.
——The organisation and laws of some Bantu tribes in East Africa. J. roy. anthrop. Inst. *45*, 1915, 234–306.
Kikuyu, Tharaka, Kamba. By far the best account of the age-grade systems and law. It is deep and thorough and conclusions are sound.
——Native laws of some Bantu tribes of East Africa. J. roy. anthrop. Inst., *51*, 1921, 217–78.
Kikuyu, Kamba, Tharaka. Not as useful as the 1915 article but still very valuable. This is a comparative account of the laws of fifteen East African Bantu tribes.

Dundas, K. R. Notes on the origin and history of the Kikuyu and Dorobo tribes. Man, *8*, 76, 1908, 136–9. [Referred to in footnotes as 1, 1908.]
Useful article on tribal history.
——Kikuyu *rika*. Man, *8*, 101, 1908, 180–2. [Referred to in footnotes as 2, 1908.]
Lists of age-grades and generation-sets.
——Kikuyu calendar. Man, *9*, 19, 1909, 37–38.
The agricultural calendar.

East African quarterly. Tribes of Ukamba: their history, customs, etc. (by J. A.). E. Afr. quart., 2, 1905, 405–13.

Eliot, *Sir* C. N. E. The East African Protectorate. London: Arnold. 1905.
Kikuyu, Kamba. A short account of little value.

Elkan, W. The East African trade in wood-carvings. Africa, *28*, 4, Oct. 1958, 314–23.

Emsheimer, E. Drei Tanzgesänge der Akamba. Ethnos, *2*, 4, 1937, 137–43.

Fazan, S. H. Land tenure in the Transkei: a guide for formulation of rules for the Kikuyu of Kenya. Afr. Stud., *3*, 2, 1944, 45–64.
Comparison of Kikuyu land system with that in Transkei.

FIDES. Une intéressante tribu du Kénya: les Bameru. Missions cath., *72*, 3325, 1940, 11–13.
Meru.

Filesi, T. Gli indigeni del Kenia ed il problema dei Mau Mau nei suoi riflessi sulla vita del paese, Universo, *36*, 1, Jan.-Feb. 1956, 15–30.

Fischer, G. A. Das Massailand. Hamburg. 1885.
Kikuyu. Fischer was the first European to cross Kikuyu, in 1883. Contains a brief account.

Fisher, Jeanne M. The anatomy of Kikuyu domesticity and husbandry. London: Dept. of Technical Co-operation. 1964.

Fitzgerald, W. Africa. London: Methuen. 1950 (7th ed. 1st ed. 1934).
A geography of Africa, with a good account of Kikuyuland.

Francis, E. C. Kenya's problems as seen by a schoolmaster in Kikuyu country. Afr. affairs, *54*, 216, July 1955, 186–95.

Francolini, B. I Kikuyu e la setta Mau Mau. Div. di Etnog., *6*, 1/4, 1953, 1–12.
——I Kikuyu e la setta Mau Mau. Riv. di Etnog., *6*, 1/4, 1953, 1–12.

Frazer, *Sir* J. Totemism and exogamy. Vol. 2, 442–6. London: Macmillan. 1910.
Meru. Contains a communication from Hobley, later reprinted in Hobley, vol. 2, 1910.

Gathigira, S. K. Mikarire ya Agikuyu [Customs of the Kikuyu]. London: Shelden Press. 1952.

Gedge, E. A recent exploration of the River Tana to Mt. Kenia. Proc. roy. geog. Soc., 1892, 513–44.
Tharaka, Meru.

Gerhold, S. Wandertage in Nordost Ukamba. Leipzig. 1903.

Ghilardi, P. Religione e credenze degli Agekoyo. Ann. lateranensi, 19, 1955, 333-48.
——La circoncisione o Irùa presso i Ghekojo. Ann. lateranensi, 20, 1956, 15–27.

Gicaru, M. Land of sunshine: scenes of life in Kenya before Mau Mau. London: Lawrence and Wishart. 1958.

Gluckman, Max. The magic of despair. *In his* Order and rebellion in tribal Africa, 137–45. London: Cohen and West. 1963.

Gourou, P. Une paysannerie africaine au milieu du XXe siècle: les Kikuyus et les crises Mau-Mau. Cah. d'outre-mer, 28, oct.-déc. 1954, 317–41.

Great Britain. Report of the East African Royal Commission, 1953–1955. London: H.M.S.O. 1955.

Gregory, J. W. The Great Rift Valley. London: Nelson. 1896.
Contains a brief and bad description of Kikuyu.

Guillain, Charles. Documents sur l'histoire, la géographie et le commerce de l'Afrique orientale. 3 vols. Paris. 1856.

Gurney, H. G. L. Appendix on the Mwimbi. *In* Kenya Mountain, *ed*. E. A. Dutton. London. 1929.
A brief but useful general account.

Guthrie, M. The classification of the Bantu languages. London: Oxford Univ. Press for Int. Afr. Inst. 1948.

Hailey, *Lord*. Kenya Colony and Protectorate. *In his* Native administration in the British African Territories, pt. 1, ch. 2. London: H.M.S.O. 1950.

Hall, B. E. F. How peace came to Kikuyu. J. Afr. Soc., *37*, 149, 1938, 423–48.
Extract of letters from Government Officer, 1892–1900. A general picture of contemporary Kikuyu.

Hildebrandt, J. M. Ethnographische Notizen über Wakamba und ihre Nachbarn. Z. f. Ethnol., *10*, 5, 1878, 347–406.
An early account, subsumed in Lindblom. 1920.

Hinde, H. *and* S. L. The last of the Masai. London. 1901.
Kikuyu. Contains a few references, of little value.

Hobley, C. W. People, prospects and places in B. E. Africa. Geog. J., 1894, 97–123.
——Kikuyu medicines. Man, *6*, 54, 1906, 81–83.
Contains lists of medicines, clans and totems.
——Notes on the Akikuyu. Man, *6*, 78, 1906, 119–20.
——Ethnology of the Akamba and other East African tribes. Cambridge Univ. Press. 1910.
Kamba, Kikuyu, Meru. Quite valuable account of Kamba; short and confused chapters on Kikuyu and Meru.
——Kikuyu customs and beliefs: *thahu* and its connection with circumcision rites. J. roy. anthrop. Inst., *40*, 1910, 428–52.
This article was absorbed into Hobley, 1922.
——Further researches in Kikuyu and Kamba religious beliefs and customs. J. roy. anthrop. Inst., *41*, 1911, 406–57.
Mostly absorbed into Hobley, 1922, except for good description of Kikuyu picture-gourd.
——Some religious beliefs of the Kikuyu and Kamba people. Report Brit. Assoc. Adv. Sci., 1911, 511–12.
Report of paper read, published in full in J.R.A.I., 1911.
——Kamba protective magic. Man, *12*, 2, 1912, 4–5.
Account of magical amulets
——Kamba game. Man, *12*, 95, 1912, 179–80.
——Bantu beliefs and magic, with particular reference to the Kikuyu and Kamba tribes of Kenya Colony. London: Witherby. 1922.
A valuable book dealing in great detail with religion and magic: it is the best account of these subjects. It was reprinted with an added final chapter in 1938.

Hofmann, J. Geburt, Heirat und Tod bei den Wakamba. Leipzig: Evang. Lutheran Mission. 1901.
Not seen, but apparently subsumed into Lindblom, 1920.

Holding, E. M. Some preliminary notes on Meru age-grades. Man, *42*, 31, 1942, 58–65.
A very useful article, with full details of age-grades, generation-sets and councils. Also valuable in giving details of women's grades and councils

Homan, F. Derek. Land consolidation and redistribution of population in the Imenti sub-tribe of the Meru (Kenya). *In* African agrarian systems, ed. Daniel Biebuyck. London: Oxford Univ. Press for Int. Afr. Inst., 1963.

Hughes, O. E B. Villages in the Kikuyu country. J. Afr. Admin., *7*, 4, Oct. 1955, 170-4.

Humphrey, N., *and others*. The Kikuyu lands. Nairobi: Govt. Printer. 1945.
Three articles on the Kikuyu Reserves, with some valuable statistical material.

Huntingford, G. W. B. The social institutions of the Dorobo Anthropos, *46*, 1/2, 1951, 1–48.
——The political organization of the Dorobo. Anthropos, *49*, 1/2, 1954, 123–48.
——The economic life of the Dorobo. Anthropos, *50*, 4/6, 1955, 602–34.
——The peopling of East Africa by its modern inhabitants. *In* History of East Africa, *eds*. R. Oliver, *and* G. Mathew, vol. I, 58–93 Oxford: Clarendon Press. 1963.

Huxley, E. Red strangers. London: Chatto & Windus. 1939.
A novel describing the effects on Kikuyu life of the coming of the Europeans. Of little value, most of the anthropological material apparently coming from Routledge.
——Kenya after Mau Mau. Optima, *7*, 3, Sept. 1957, 101–9.

Itotia, Justin. Kikuyu customs. Nairobi, 1937.

Jackson, *Sir* F. Early days in East Africa. London: Arnold. 1930.
A few references to Kikuyu.

Johnstone, H. B. Notes on the tribes occupying Mombasa subdistrict, British East Africa. J. roy anthrop. Inst., *32*, 1902, 263–72.
Contains some notes on the Kamba living near the coast.

Joyce, T. A. Note on a series of Kikuyu "ndomi" in the British Museum. Man, *6*, 33, 1906, 49–51.
Description of dancing shields.

Kabuti, K. African marriage systems [Kikuyu]. Indo-Asian culture, *6*, 3, Jan. 1958, 299–309.

Kenya. Native land tenure in Kikuyu Province: report of Committee, November 1929, with appendix (Chairman G. V. Maxwell). 1930.
The report covers all aspects of land tenure among all Kikuyu tribes The material is full and factual: a most valuable account.

Kenya. Kenya Land Commission, 1932: report and evidence. 3 vols. Nairobi: Govt. Printer. 1933 [also London: H.M.S.O. (Colonial no. 91) 1934].
Vol. 1. Kikuyu. 2. Kamba. The Commission was concerned principally with the alienation of land to Europeans. As a sociological account it is not very good, but it contains much statistical and general information and has a vivid account of the taking of Kikuyu land for European farms. Referred to in text as K.L.C. report on evidence.

Kenyatta, J. Kikuyu religion, ancestor worship and sacrificial practices. Africa, *10*, 3, July 1937, 308–28.
Enlarged and reprinted in his *Facing Mount Kenya*. 1938.
——My people of Kenya. London: U.S.C.L. 1942.
Kikuyu. A small popularly written booklet. Nothing not in Kenyatta 1938.
——Facing Mount Kenya. London: Secker & Warburg. 1938 [2nd ed. 1953].
Kikuyu. With Routledge, the best monograph on the Kikuyu, containing the best account of Kikuyu social organization in the literature.

Kilson, M. L. Land and the Kikuyu: a study of the relationships between land and Kikuyu political movements. J. Negro Hist., *40*, 2, Apr. 1955, 103–53.

König, B. Dornige Pfade eines jungen Missionar in Ukamba. Leipzig. 1902.

Kolb, G. Von Mombasa durch Ukambani zum Kenia. Petermanns Mitt., 42, 1896, 221–31.
——Im Lande der Wakamba. Luth. Missionsbl., 1898.

Kolbe, L. H., *and* Fouche, S. F. Land consolidation and farm planning in the Central Province [Kikuyu]. Nairobi: Kenya Dept of Agriculture. 1959.

Krapf. J. L. Travels, researches and missionary labours, during an eighteen years' residence in eastern Africa. London: Trübner. 1860.
Contains some interesting material on the Kamba; he was the first European to visit their country, and had close contact with the Kamba settlements near the coast.

Lambert, H. E. The use of indigenous authorities in tribal administration: studies of the Meru of Kenya Colony. Univ. Cape Town (Communications School Afr. Stud., 16, 1947).
A good account of Meru political organization. Most of the paper is concerned with modern administrative problems, but it contains much concise and detailed material.
——Land tenure among the Akamba. Afr. Stud., *6*, 3, 1947, p. 131; 4, p. 157.
The fullest account on land tenure, with good material on social organization, ritual, etc. A valuable source of information [Referred to in footnotes as 2, 1947.]
——The systems of land tenure in the Kikuyu land unit. Univ. Cape Town (Communications School Afr. Stud., 22, 1950).
A full account of the history and traditions of the Kikuyu and northern tribes, including their account of the origins of their land systems. Summarizes earlier accounts on these subjects.
——The background to Mau Mau: widespread use of secret oaths in Kenya. Times Brit. colonies Rev., 8, winter 1952, p. 21.
——Kikuyu social and political institutions. London: Oxford Univ. Press. 1956.

Larby, N. The Kamba. Nairobi: C.M.S. 1944.
A short account, not of great value.

Laughton, W. H. The Meru. Nairobi: C.M.S. 1944.
A short account.

Leakey, L. S. B. The Kikuyu problem of the initiation of girls. J. roy anthrop. Inst., *61*, 1931, 277–85.
A short account of pre-marital sexual behaviour and the significance of girls' initiation.
——Some aspects of the Kikuyu tribe. Man, *34*, 72, 1934, p. 59.
Brief summary of lecture.
——Some problems arising from the part played by goats and sheep in the social life of the Akikuyu. J. Afr. Soc., *33*, 130, 1934, 70-79.
Short article on social value of livestock.
——Mau Mau and the Kikuyu. London: Methuen. 1952.
Popular account, includes a good general description of Kikuyu; chapter on social organization clears up much that is confusing in other available material.
——Defeating Mau Mau. London: Methuen. 1954.
——Mau Mau as a religion. Manchester Guardian, 24, 25, June 1954.
——New ways for the Kikuyu. 1. Village life. 2. Land consolidation. Manchester Guardian, 4, 12, Dec. 1956.

Leys, N. M., *and* Joyce, T. A. Notes on a series of physical measurements from East Africa [Kikuyu, Kamba and Embu]. J. roy. anthrop. Inst., *43*, 1913, 195–267.

Lindblom, G. Kriggföring och därmed förbundra bruk bland Kamba-negerns i Brittiska Ost Afrika. Ymer, 24, 1914, 123–37.
——Outlines of a Tharaka grammar. Uppsala. 1914.
——Tron pa den magiska kraften hos namm bland Kamba-negerns i Ostafrika. Ymer, *37*, 3–4, 1917.
——"Svart" magi och skyddsatgärder mot dylik hos Akamba i Ostafrika. Ymer, *37*, 2, 1917.
——The Akamba in British East Africa. Uppsala: Appelberg. 1920.
The best general account of the Kamba. Lindblom was a trained ethnographer, and although the book is weak on social organization, it is full on most aspects of Kamba life, and altogether a very considerable work.
——Notes on the Kamba language. Uppsala: Appelberg. 1925.
——Die Beschneidung bei den Akamba. Völkerkunde, *3*, 4/6, 1927, 100–8.
——Kamba folklore. 1. Tales of animals. Uppsala: Appelberg, 1928.
Legends and stories, with ethnographic notes.
——Kamba riddles, proverbs and songs. Uppsala: Appelberg. 1934.
——Kamba folklore. 2. Tales of supernatural beings and adventures. Uppsala: Appelberg. 1935.
Legends and stories, with ethnographic notes.

Liversage, V. Land tenure in the colonies. Cambridge Univ. Press. 1945.
Contains some useful references to Kikuyu land tenure.

Low, D. A. The northern interior, 1840–1884. *In* History of East Africa, *eds.* R. Oliver, *and* G. Mathew, vol. I, 297–351. Oxford: Clarendon Press. 1963.

Lugard, F. D. The rise of our East African empire. 2 vols. Edinburgh, London: Blackwood, 1893.
Vol. 1 contains a few references to the Kikuyu.

Lyn-Watt, R. Stall feeding of goats and sheep by the Kikuyu tribe. E. Afr. agric. J., 8, 1942–3, 109–11.

MacDermott, P. L. British East Africa or IBEA. London. 1885.
Contains a few notes on the Kikuyu.

MacDonald, J. R. L. Soldiering and surveying in British East Africa, 1891-1894. London. 1897.
Contains a few notes on the Kikuyu.

McGregor, A. W. Kikuyu and its peoples. Church missionary Rev., 1909.

MacKinder, H. J. A journey to the summit of Mount Kenya. Geog. J., *15*, 1900, 453–86.
Contains a few useful references.

Maher, C. Soil erosion and land utilization in the Ukamba (Kitui) Reserve. 2 vols. Mimeographed. Nairobi: Govt. of Kenya. 1937.
——A note on economic and social problems in Kenya and their relationship to soil erosion. C.R. INCIDI, 25, annexe 2, 1949, 63–72.

Makerere College: Kikuyu Embu and Meru Students Association. Around Mount Kenya: comment on Corfield. 1960.

Matheson, A. Na de Mau Mau een nieuwe toekomst voor de Kikuyu's. Meded. Afr. Inst., *10*, 9, Sept. 1956, 258–62.

Maxwell Report, *see under* Kenya.

Middleton, J. The Kikuyu and Kamba of Kenya. London: Int. Afr. Inst. 1953.
——Les Kikouyou et les Kamba du Kenia. Paris: Payot. 1954.
——Kenya: administration and changes in African life, 1912–1945. *In* History of East Africa, *eds.* V. Harlow, *and* E. M. Chilver, 1965, vol. 2. Oxford: Clarendon Press.

Mockerie, P. G. An African speaks for his people. London: Hogarth Press. 1934.
——The life of an African teacher. *In* Ten Africans, *ed.* M. Perham, London, 1963 (new ed).
Kikuyu. Popular non-sociological accounts of little use.

Moreau, R. E. Joking relationship (*utani*) in Tanganyika. Tanganyika notes, 14, 1941, pp. 1–10.

Murphy, J. H. B. The Kitui Kamba: further investigation on certain matters. J. roy. anthrop. Inst., *56*, 1926, 195–206.
Useful notes on *kithitu* and on spirit possession. [Referred to in footnotes as 1, 1926.]
——The "Kithito" at Mivukomi, Mumoni district, Kenya Colony. Man. *26*, 135, 1926, p. 207.
Kamba. Notes on a *kithitu*.

Needham, R. The left hand of the Mugwe. Africa, *30*, 1, Jan. 1960, 20–33.

Neligan, C. W. Description of *kijesu* ceremony among the Akamba, Tiva river, East Africa. Man, *11*, 34, 1911, p. 49.
Description of a spirit possession.

Norden, H. White and black in East Africa. London: Witherby. 1924.
Kikuyu, Kamba. Poor accounts.

Nottingham, J. C. Sorcery in Kenya. J. Afr. Admin., *11*, 1, Jan. 1959, 2–14.

Orde-Browne, G. St. J. Circumcision ceremonies among the Amwimbe. Man, *13*, 79, 1913, 137–40.
Detailed description of a ceremony.
——The circumcision ceremony in Chuka. Man, *15*, 39, 1915, 65–68.
Detailed description of a ceremony.
——Mount Kenya and its peoples: some notes on the Chuka tribe. J. Afr. Soc., *15*, 59, 1916, 225–31.
——The vanishing tribes of Kenya. London: Seeley, Service & Co. 1925.
Northern tribes. Although a semi-popular account, this is a valuable book; it covers all aspects of the culture of these otherwise little documented tribes, and is especially full on material culture.

Orr, J. B., *and* Gilks, J. L. Studies of nutrition: the physique and health of two African tribes. London: H.M.S.O. (Med. Research Council, Special Report ser. 155).
Kikuyu. Contains useful data on Kikuyu diet, as compared with that of the Masai.

Pant, Apa B. Social disintegration of the African native. United Asia, *7*, 2, Mar. 1955, 94–96.

Parapini, G. Fra i Kamba del Kenia. Universo, *38*, 1, Jan.-Feb. 1958, 45–56.

Patterson, J. H. In the grip of the Nyika. London. 1909.
Meru. A popular account with a few references.

Pedraza, G. J. W. Land consolidation in the Kikuyu areas of Kenya. J. Afr. Admin., *8*, 2, Apr. 1956, 82–87.

Penwill, D. J. Kamba customary law: notes taken in the Machakos District of Kenya colony. London: Macmillan. 1950.
A very useful summary of all aspects of Kamba law; contains little new, but makes some corrections to earlier accounts.
——A pilot scheme for two Kikuyu improved villages near Nairobi. J. Afr. Admin., *12*, 2, Apr. 1960, 61–67.

Perham, M. Kenya after Mau Mau. Corona, *9*, 3, Mar. 1957, 252–4.

Peters, C., *tr.* Dulcken, H. W. New light on dark Africa: a narrative of the German Emin Pasha expedition . . . London. 1891.
Contains a few references to the Kikuyu.

Phillips, A. Report on native tribunals. Nairobi: Govt. Printer. 1945.
Kikuyu, Kamba, Northern tribes. Has many valuable references to the political organization of these tribes, but concerned primarily with the reorganization of the modern tribunal system. Based on official documents.

Philp, H. R. A. New day in Kenya. London. 1936.
Short account of missionary activities.

Powell-Cotton, P. H. G. In unknown Africa. London. 1904.
Kikuyu. A few references, apparently taken from Routledge, whom the author met.

Prins, A. H. J. The coastal tribes of the North-eastern Bantu. London: Int. Afr. Inst. 1952.
——Mau-Mau als ontspoord reveil. Meded. Afr. Inst., *9*, 5, 1955, 115–19.

Proctor, R. A. The Kikuyu market and Kikuyu diet. Kenya med. J., 3, 1926, 15–22.

Radcliffe-Brown, A. R. Primitive law. Encyclopaedia of social sciences, vol. 9, 1933.
——Taboo (Frazer lecture). Cambridge Univ. Press. 1939.

Rath, J. T. Mau-Mau das warnende Zeichen. Z. Missionswiss. u. Religionswiss., *39*, 4, 1955, 297–316.

Rawcliffe, D. H. The struggle for Kenya. London: Gollancz. 1954.

Rawson, D. C. Background of the Mau-Mau. Natural Hist., *63*, 7, Sept. 1954, 296–302.

Rosenstiel, A. An anthropological approach to the Mau Mau problem. Polit. Sci. quart., Sept. 1953, 419–32.

Routledge, W. S. *and* K. An Akikuyu image. Man, *6*, 1, 1906, 1–3.
——With a prehistoric people: The Akikuyu, based on five years' fieldwork in Nyeri. London. 1910
The first monograph on the Kikuyu, based on five years' fieldwork in Nyeri. The authors were trained in anthropology. The book is weak on social organization but has good chapters on religion. The sections on material culture and technology are detailed and well illustrated.

Royal Anthropological Institute. A Mkamba *mwanake* (warrior). Man, *31*, 268, Dec. 1931, 278–9.

Säuberlich, G. Article in Jb. sächsischen Missionskonf., Leipzig, 1899. [Kamba.]

Schapera, I. Some problems of anthropological research in Kenya Colony. London. 1949.
Contains a bibliography of published and unpublished material on all tribes.

Shackleton, E. R. The Njuwe. Man, *30*, 143, 1930, p. 201.
Tharaka. Brief note on an extinct people formerly living in Tharaka.

Shannon, M. I. Rehabilitating the Kikuyu. Afr. affairs, *54*, 215, Apr. 1955, 129–37.
——Rebuilding the social life of the Kikuyu. Afr. affairs, *56*, 225, Oct. 1957, 276–84.
——Social revolution in Kikuyu-land: rehabilitation and welfare work in Kenya's new village communities. Afr. world, Sept. 1955, 7–9; Oct. 1955, 11–12.

Simmance, A. J. F. The adoption of children among the Kikuyu of Kiambu District. J. Afr. law, *3*, 1, spring 1959, 33–38.

Slater, M. The trial of Jomo Kenyatta. London: Secker and Warburg. 1955.

Southall, A. W. Population movements in East Africa. *In* Essays on African population, *eds.* K. M. Barbour, *and* R. M. Prothero. London: Kegan Paul. 1961.

Stanner, W. E. H. The Kitui Kamba: a critical study of British administration (unpublished MS.). 1938.

Stannus, H. Pre-Bantu occupants of East Africa. Man, *15*, 76, 1915, 131–2.

Stigand, C. H. The land of Zinj. London: Constable. 1913.
Kikuyu. Has good description of the country and list of miscellaneous customs. Nothing new.

Stoneham, C. T. Mau Mau. London: Museum Press. 1953.

Tate, H. R. Notes on the Kikuyu and Kamba tribes of East Africa. J. roy. anthrop. Inst. *34*, 1904, 130–48, 255–66. [Referred to in footnotes as 1, 1904, and 2, 1904.]
Good account of dress and ornaments, material culture and technology.
——The native law of the southern Gikuyu of British East Africa. *J. Afr. Soc.*, *9*, 35, 1910, 233–54; *10*, 39, 1911, 285–97.
Useful articles with details of legal procedure, list of kinship terms, age-set and generation-set names.
——Kikuyu *thathi*. J. E. Afr. Ug. nat. Hist. Soc., *6*, 1918, 261–5.
Description of oaths.

Thomson, J. Through Masailand. London: Sampson Law. 1885 (2nd ed.).
A few references to Kikuyu.

Thorp, J. K. R. African beekeepers: notes on the methods and customs relating to the bee-culture of the Akamba tribe in Kenya Colony. J. E. Afr. Ug. nat. Hist. Soc., *17*, 1943, 255–73.

Times, The. Agrarian revolution at work in Kikuyuland. Times brit. colonies Rev., 2, **1957**, p. **12**.

Villaret, F. Jomo Kenyatta et le mouvement de revendication indigène au Kenya. Rev. polit. et parlementaire, *57*, 645, fév. 1955, 176–83.

von Höhnel, L., *tr*. Bell, N. The discovery of Lakes Rudolf and Stefanie. 2 vols. London. **1894**. Kikuyu, Northern Tribes. Vol. 1. contains a good account of the country and people. Teleki and von Höhnel were the first Europeans to cross North Kikuyu.

Wakefield, T. Routes of native caravans from the coast to the interior of eastern Africa. J. roy. geog. Soc., *40*, 1870, 303–28.

Watt, S. In the heart of savagedom. London and Glasgow: Pickering and Inglis. 1912.

Welbourn, F. B. East African rebels: a study of some independent churches. London. SCM Press. 1961.

Werner, A. The Akikuyu. J. Afr. Soc., *10*, 40, 1911, 447–58.
A review of Routledge, 1910, but with comparative material added. Of no value.

Whiteley, W. H., *and* Gutkind, A. E. A linguistic bibliography of East Africa. Kampala: East African Institute of Social Research. 1958 (rev. ed.).

Wiseman, E. M. Kikuyu martyrs, London: Highway Press, 1958.

INDEX

Other Titles in this Series

WESTERN AFRICA

Part I — THE AKAN AND GA-ADANGME PEOPLES, by Madeline Manoukian. Pp. 108, map. 12*s.* 6*d.*

Part II — THE PEOPLES OF SIERRA LEONE, by Merran McCulloch. Pp. 102, map. 12*s.* 6*d.*

Part III — THE IBO AND IBIBIO-SPEAKING PEOPLES OF SOUTH-EASTERN NIGERIA, by Daryll Forde and G. I. Jones. Pp. 80, map. 7*s.* 6*d.*

Part IV — THE YORUBA-SPEAKING PEOPLES OF SOUTH-WESTERN NIGERIA, by Daryll Forde. Pp. 102, map. 8*s.* 6*d.*

Part V — TRIBES OF THE NORTHERN TERRITORIES OF THE GOLD COAST, by Madeline Manoukian. Pp. 102, map. (Out of print.)

Part VI — THE EWE-SPEAKING PEOPLE OF TOGOLAND AND THE GOLD COAST, by Madeline Manoukian. Pp. 61, map. (Out of print.)

Part VII — PEOPLES OF THE PLATEAU AREA OF NORTHERN NIGERIA, by Harold D. Gunn. Pp. 111, map. (Out of print.)

Part VIII — THE TIV OF CENTRAL NIGERIA, by Laura and Paul Bohannan. Pp. 100, map. 9*s.* 6*d.*

Part IX — PEOPLES OF THE CENTRAL CAMEROONS: TIKAR, by Merran McCulloch; BAMUM AND BAMILEKE, by Margaret Littlewood; BANEN, BAFIA, AND BALOM, by I. Dugast. Pp. 172, map. (Out of print.)

Part X — PEOPLES OF THE NIGER-BENUE CONFLUENCE: NUPE, by Daryll Forde; IGBIRA, by Paula Brown; IGALA and IDOMA-SPEAKING PEOPLES, by Robert G. Armstrong. Pp. 160, maps. (Out of print.)

Part XI — COASTAL BANTU OF THE CAMEROONS, by Edwin Ardener. Pp. 116, maps. (Out of print.)

Part XII — PAGAN PEOPLES OF THE CENTRAL AREA OF NORTHERN NIGERIA, by Harold D. Gunn. Pp. 147, map. 17*s.* 6*d.*

Part XIII — THE BENIN KINGDOM AND THE EDO-SPEAKING PEOPLES OF SOUTH-WESTERN NIGERIA, by R. E. Bradbury, together with a section on the ITSEKIRI, by P. C. Lloyd. Pp. 212, maps. 25*s.* 0*d.*

Part XIV — THE WOLOF OF SENEGAMBIA, by David P. Gamble. Pp. 100, maps. 16*s.* 0*d.*

Part XV — PEOPLES OF THE MIDDLE NIGER REGION OF NORTHERN NIGERIA, by Harold D. Gunn and F. P. Conant. Pp. 141, map. 17*s.* 6*d.*

French Series

Part I — LES BAMBARA, by Viviana Pâques. Pp. viii, 123 map. 15*s.* 9*d.*

Part II — LES SONGHAY, by Jean Rouch. Pp. vii, 100, map. 14*s.* 0*d.*

Part III — LES CONIAGUI ET LES BASSARI, by Monique de Lestrange. Pp. vi, 86, diagrams, map. 14*s.* 0*d.*

Part IV — LES DOGON, by Montserrat Palau Marti. Pp. xii, 122, maps. 17*s.* 6*d.*

Part V — LES SÉNOUFO, by B. Holas. Pp. viii, 183, map. (Out of print.)

Part VI — LE GROUPE DIT PAHOUIN (FANG-BOULOU-BETI) by P. Alexandre and J. Binet. Pp. vi, 152, map. 17*s.* 6*d.*

Part VII — LES KONGO NORD-OCCIDENTAUX, by Marcel Soref. Pp. viii, 144, map. 21*s.* 0*d.*

Part VIII — LES POPULATIONS DU TCHAD, by Annie M.-D. Lebeuf. Pp. 130, map. (Out of print.)

Part IX — LES POPULATIONS PAIENNES DU NORD CAMEROUN ET DE L'ADAMAOUA, by B. Lembezat. Pp. 252, map. 35*s.* 0*d.*

Part X LES POPULATIONS DU NORD-TOGO, by J.-C. Froelich, P. Alexandre and R. Cornevin. Pp. 195, map. 37s. 6d.

Published for the Institute by the Presses Universitaires de France, Paris.

NORTH-EASTERN AFRICA

Part I PEOPLES OF THE HORN OF AFRICA: SOMALI, AFAR, AND SAHO, by I. M. Lewis. Pp. 200, map. (Out of print.)

Part II THE GALLA OF ETHIOPIA: THE KINGDOMS OF KAFA AND JANJERO, by G. W. B. Huntingford. Pp. 156, maps. (Out of print.)

Part III PEOPLES OF SOUTH-WEST ETHIOPIA AND ITS BORDERLAND, by Ernesta Ceruli. Pp. 148, maps. (Out of print.)

EAST CENTRAL AFRICA

Part I PEOPLES OF THE LAKE NYASA REGION, by Mary Tew. Pp. 156, diagrams, map. (Out of print.)

Part II BEMBA AND RELATED PEOPLES OF NORTHERN RHODESIA, by Wilfred Whiteley; PEOPLES OF THE LUAPULA VALLEY, by J. Slaski. Pp. 100, maps. (Out of print.)

Part III THE COASTAL TRIBES OF THE NORTH-EASTERN BANTU: POKOMO, NYIKA AND TEITA, by A. H. J. Prins. Pp. 138, map. (Out of print.)

Part IV THE NILOTES OF THE SUDAN AND UGANDA, by Audrey J. Butt. Pp. 198, map. 20s. 0d.

Part V THE KIKUYU AND KAMBA OF KENYA, by John Middleton and Greet Kershaw. Pp. 103, map. 20s. 0d.

Part VI THE NORTHERN NILO-HAMITES, by G. W. B. Huntingford. Pp. 106, diagrams, maps. 13s. 0d.

Part VII THE CENTRAL NILO-HAMITES, by Pamela Gulliver and P. H. Gulliver. Pp. 103, diagrams, maps. (Out of print.)

Part VIII THE SOUTHERN NILO-HAMITES, by G. W. B. Huntingford. Pp. 152, diagrams, maps. (Out of print.)

Part IX THE AZANDE AND RELATED PEOPLES OF THE ANGLO-EGYPTIAN SUDAN AND BELGIAN CONGO, by P. T. W. Baxter and Audrey Butt. Pp. 150. map. (Out of print.)

Part X THE GISU OF UGANDA, by J. S. La Fontaine. Pp. 68, maps. 9s. 6d.

Part XI THE EASTERN LACUSTRINE BANTU (GANDA, SOGA, &c.), by Margaret Chave Fallers. 12s. 6d.

Part XII THE SWAHILI-SPEAKING PEOPLES OF ZANZIBAR AND THE EAST AFRICAN COAST, by A. H. J. Prins. Pp. 143, map, diagrams. 21s. 0d.

Part XIII THE WESTERN LACUSTRINE BANTU (NYORO, TORO, &c.), by Brian K. Taylor, Pp. 159, maps. 21s. 0d.

Part XIV LES ANCIENS ROYAUMES DE LA ZONE INTER-LACUSTRE MÉRIDIONALE, by A. A. Trouwborst. M. d'Hertefelt and J. H. Scherer. (Also published in the series: Annales du Musée Royal de l'Afrique Centrale, Monographies ethnographiques.) Pp. viii, 252, maps. 27s. 0d.

MADAGASCAR

Part I LES MALGACHES DU SUD-EST, by Hubert Deschamps and Suzanne Vianès. Pp. x, 118, map, plates. 16s. 0d.

WEST CENTRAL AFRICA

Part I THE SOUTHERN LUNDA AND RELATED PEOPLES (NORTHERN RHODESIA, ANGOLA, BELGIAN CONGO), by Merran McCulloch. Pp. 110, map. (Out of print.)

Part II The Ovimbundu of Angola, by Merran McCulloch. Pp. 50, diagrams, map. (Out of print.)

Part III The Lozi Peoples of North-Western Rhodesia, by V. W. Turner. Pp. 64, map. 7*s*. 6*d*.

Part IV The Ila-Tonga Peoples of North-Western Rhodesia, by M. A. Jaspan. Pp. 72, map. 8*s*. 6*d*.

CONGO

Part I Les Tribus Ba-Kuba et les Peuplades Apparentées, by J. Vansina. Pp. ix, 64, map. 8*s*. 6*d*.

Part II Les Bira et les Peuplades Limitrophes, by H. Van Geluwe. Pp. xii, 165, map. 17*s*. 6*d*.

Part III Les Mamvu-Mangutu et Balese-Mvuba, by H. Van Geluwe. Pp. xv, 195, map. 21*s*. 0*d*.

Part IV Les Peuplades de L'Entre Congo-Ubangui (Ngbandi, Ngbaka, Mbandja, Ngambe et Gens d'Eau), by H. Burssens. Pp. xi, 219, map. 21*s*. 0*d*.

Part V Les Bali et les Peuplades Apparentées (Ndaka-Mbo-Beke-Lika-Budu-Nyari), by H. Van Geluwe. Pp. ix, 130, map. 17*s*. 6*d*.

(Also published in the series: Annales du Musée Royale d l'Afrique Centrale Monographies ethnographiques.)

SOUTHERN AFRICA

Part I The Swazi, by Hilda Kuper. Pp. 89, map. (Out of print.)

Part II The Southern Sotho, by V. G. J. Sheddick. Pp. 86, map. 8*s*. 6*d*.

Part III The Tswana, by I. Schapera. Pp. 77, map. 8*s*. 6*d*.

Part IV The Shona and Ndebele of Southern Rhodesia, by Hilda Kuper, A. J. B. Hughes and J. Van Velsen. Pp. 128, map. 15*s*. 0*d*.